THE ___S DEBATE

General Editor: Michael Scott

D1368913

23627

The Critics Debate

General Editor Michael Scott

Published titles

Sons and Lovers   Geoffrey Harvey
Bleak House   Jeremy Hawthorn
The Canterbury Tales   Alcuin Blamires
Tess of the d'Urbervilles   Terence Wright
The Waste Land and Ash Wednesday   Arnold P. Hinchliffe
Paradise Lost   Margarita Stocker
King Lear   Ann Thompson
Othello   Peter Davison
The Winter's Tale   Bill Overton
Gulliver's Travels   Brian Tippett
Blake: Songs of Innocence and Experience   David Lindsay
Measure for Measure   T.F. Wharton
Hamlet   Michael Hattaway
The Tempest   David Daniell
Coriolanus   Bruce King
Wuthering Heights   Peter Miles
The Metaphysical Poets   Donald Mackenzie
The Great Gatsby   Stephen Matterson
Heart of Darkness   Robert Burden
To the Lighthouse   Su Reid
Portrait of a Lady/Turn of the Screw   David Kirby
Hard Times   Allen Samuels
Philip Larkin   Stephen Regan

Further titles are in preparation

PHILIP LARKIN

Stephen Regan

MACMILLAN

First published 1992 by
MACMILLAN EDUCATION LTD
Houndmills, Basingstoke, Hampshire RG21 2XS
and London
Companies and representatives
throughout the world

ISBN 0–333–47496–1 hardcover
ISBN 0–333–47497–X paperback

A catalogue record for this book is available
from the British Library.

Typeset by Footnote Graphics,
Warminster, Wiltshire
Printed in Hong Kong

Contents

For Gaynor

General Editor's Preface

OVER THE last few years the practice of literary criticism has become hotly debated. Methods developed earlier in the century and before have been attacked and the word 'crisis' has been drawn upon to describe the present condition of English Studies. That such a debate is taking place is a sign of the subject discipline's health. Some would hold that the situation necessitates a radical alternative approach which naturally implies a 'crisis situation'. Others would respond that to employ such terms is to precipitate or construct a false position. The debate continues but it is not the first. 'New Criticism' acquired its title because it attempted something fresh, calling into question certain practices of the past. Yet the practices it attacked were not entirely lost or negated by the new critics. One factor becomes clear: English Studies is a pluralistic discipline.

What are students coming to advanced work in English for the first time to make of all this debate and controversy? They are in danger of being overwhelmed by the cross-currents of critical approaches as they take up their study of literature. The purpose of this series is to help delineate various critical approaches to specific literary texts. Its authors are from a variety of critical schools and have approached their task in a flexible manner. Their aim is to help the reader come to terms with the variety of criticism and to introduce him or her to further reading on the subject and to a fuller evaluation of a particular text by illustrating the way it has been approached in a number of contexts. In the first part of the book a critical survey is given of some of the major ways the text has been appraised. This is done sometimes in a thematic manner, sometimes according to various 'schools' or 'approaches'. In the second part the authors provide their own appraisals of the text from their stated critical standpoint, allowing the reader the knowledge of their own particular approaches from which their views may in turn be evaluated. The series therein hopes to introduce and to elucidate criticism of authors and texts being studied and to encourage participation as the critics debate.

Michael Scott

Acknowledgements

The author and publishers wish to thank Faber and Faber Ltd for permission to use copyright material from *Collected Poems* by Philip Larkin.

Every effort has been made to trace all the copyright holders, but if any have been inadvertently overlooked the publishers will be pleased to make the necessary arrangement at the first opportunity.

Introduction

THE POETRY of Philip Larkin might seem an unlikely choice of
subject for a series of books exploring the current critical debate in
literary studies. There is no well-established critical tradition to
compare with that of earlier writers, for instance, and no obvious
theoretical divisions in which to place existing interpretations of
Larkin's work. Larkin's poetry remains untouched by some of the
most recent developments in critical theory. There is, nevertheless, a
diversity of critical opinion about Larkin's achievements as a writer
and this continues to inform a lively and often fierce debate about
the scope and direction of twentieth-century poetry. There is also
evidence in recent Larkin scholarship of a new interest in linguistic
analysis and a determination to move beyond the old-fashioned
thematic criticism that has dominated the teaching of English
literature for so long. These new perspectives and approaches will
undoubtedly stimulate further debate and lead in time to a radical
reappraisal of Larkin's work.

As Part One of this study suggests, the predominantly formalist
and thematic criticism of the 1960s rarely questioned the ideas and
assumptions at work in Larkin's poetry and tended to accept its
implicit world view as a modest and tolerant assessment of our
common 'human condition'. There were two strong voices of dissent
in the early years of Larkin criticism, but both Alfred Alvarez and
Charles Tomlinson formulated their objections to Larkin's work in
terms of a preference for the more urgent, experimental poetry being
produced by modern American writers, rather than seeking to
understand the poetry in terms of its own context. When critics like
Donald Davie came to Larkin's defence, it was usually to stress the
social realism of the poetry and its clear-sighted acceptance of 'the
way things were'. Such criticism was well intentioned but did little
to persuade Larkin's detractors of the value of his work. Instead,
Larkin came to be seen, in derogatory terms, as the reluctant

laureate of the drab and austere surfaces of post-war Britain, 'a sad-faced poet all Kodaks and lost chances', as one critic called him (Grubb, 1965, p.226). Significantly, though, it was this image of ordinariness and accessibility which, like that of John Betjeman, served to recommend Larkin to a contemporary readership and helped to sustain his popularity.

The publication of *High Windows* in 1974 seemed calculated to confound the earlier critical assessment of Larkin's work and the increasingly familiar charges that the poetry was beset with bore-dom, mediocrity and compromise, and that it relied too heavily on a narrow range of traditional forms and techniques. After 1974 the critical response to Larkin's poetry shifted drastically; Larkin came to be seen as a much more provocative, disquieting and 'difficult' writer than previously, and critics began to perceive in his work the impact of European modernism and symbolism. The old charges of 'gentility' and 'parochialism' were put to flight.

In its survey of critical trends, Part One of this book asks what relevance, if any, might be attached to Larkin's role in the so-called 'Movement' in the 1950s. Part One also considers the claims of those critics who have attempted to 'place' Larkin's work within estab-lished literary traditions such as Romanticism, Realism, Modernism and Symbolism. Larkin has been variously identified as the natural successor to Wordsworth, Hardy and Edward Thomas, and more recently as the surreptitious follower of Yeats, Eliot and Lawrence. Part Two goes against the grain by arguing that the most significant and lasting 'influence' on Larkin's work was the poetry of the 1930s, especially that of W.H. Auden and Louis MacNeice. Attempts to categorise Larkin as a late Romantic or an unacknowledged Mod-ernist have tended to prise his work away from its own formative context, as if the events and circumstances of the time were too dull and dreary to contemplate. This study argues to the contrary that any responsible criticism of Larkin's work must ultimately acknow-ledge the crucial importance of the changing social and cultural context in which the poetry was written and in which it continues to be read. As a contribution to the critical debate, Part Two offers a detailed analysis of Larkin's wartime writing and goes on to explore the language of the poems in terms of the tensions and conflicts which are still evident in post-war British politics. For ease of reference, Part Two discusses the poems as they appeared in individual collections from *The Less Deceived* to *High Windows*, but it also provides page numbers for readers using Anthony Thwaite's edition of the *Collected Poems*, published jointly by The Marvell Press and Faber and Faber in 1988.

Part One: Survey

Philip Larkin and the Movement

Discussions about poetic groups and movements are often confusing and misleading. Some critics have a tendency to approach literary history with simple formulas or convenient labels, thereby effacing the complex social and cultural dimensions of particular literary works. In the case of Philip Larkin, a good deal of critical debate has been concerned with the existence – real or imagined – of a group of writers known as the Movement. The common assumption is that the Movement was largely a reaction against the inflated romanticism of the 1940s, a victory of common sense and clarity over obscurity and mystification, of verbal restraint over stylistic excess: in short, the virtues of Philip Larkin over those of Dylan Thomas. Those critics who admire the rationalism of Larkin's verse have been concerned to emphasise the importance of the Movement and its continuing influence in contemporary poetry; some have gone so far as to claim for the Movement a significant place in a tradition of modern poetry – usually dubbed 'the English line' – extending back through Edward Thomas and Thomas Hardy to the poetry of William Wordsworth.

At the same time, there exists a degree of scepticism about the aims and achievements of the Movement. John Press, surveying the poetry of the 1950s, finds the issue unsettling: 'To what extent the Movement was more than a lively journalistic invention is not easy to decide' (Press, 1969, p.253). Ian Hamilton concludes that the movement was a 'hard-sell' by the literary journals on behalf of a favoured few: 'it was a take-over bid and it brilliantly succeeded' (Hamilton, 1972, p.71). This critical scepticism is compounded by the reluctance of the writers themselves to acknowledge their membership of a particular group. Larkin, when interviewed by

Hamilton, confessed 'no sense at all' of belonging to a movement, and Thom Gunn has said of the Movement: 'I found I was in it before I knew it existed ... and I have a certain suspicion that it does *not* exist' (Morrison, 1980, p.4).

If the Movement did not exist as a coherent literary group, it certainly operated as a significant cultural influence; it was the product of specific views about literature and society, which in turn it helped to establish and disseminate. What is important here is not to demonstrate that the Movement was a well-organised group with a clear and consistent programme of ideas, but rather to recognise it as a shared set of values and assumptions closely related to the moods and conditions of post-war England. To understand the origins of the Movement and its relationship with Larkin's poetry it is necessary to return to the autumn of 1954 when the arrival of a new poetic trend was announced in the literary journals.

What emerges most forcefully from the early articles and reviews announcing 'the Movement' is not so much a departure from the alleged romanticism of the 1940s as an awareness of the continuing dominance of W.H. Auden and the poets of the 1930s. In his review article, 'Poets of the Fifties' (generally thought to herald the Movement), Anthony Hartley begins by asking 'What do most readers mean when they talk of modern poetry?' He offers the following reply:

> In the eyes of the general reader it is the Thirties that continue to typify the modern movement in verse ... Now, however, there are signs that this twenty-year old domination is coming to an end. New names in the reviews, a fresh atmosphere of controversy, a new spirit of criticism – these are signs that some other group of poets is appearing on the horizon. (Hartley, 1954, p.260)

At the same time as signalling a shift in direction, the new poetry retains its roots in the work of the 1930s. In Hartley's estimation, 'the return to romanticism which came between was essentially a sport'. Hartley does not consider the new movement to be a school of poets with a specific programme and manifesto, but there is evidence, he argues, 'that the present generation has been sufficiently affected by common influences and circumstances for a not too vague *zeitgeist* to be apparent in their productions' (Hartley, 1954, p.260). 'Poets of the Fifties' is perhaps the earliest and the most useful description of the Movement as it was perceived in its own time, but few critics have since bothered to identity the 'common influences and circumstances' that its author alludes to.

Hartley, in fact, goes some way towards explaining the characteristic features of the new poetry: 'It might roughly be described as "dissenting" and non-conformist, cool, scientific and analytical . . . the poetic equivalent of liberal, dissenting England' (Hartley, 1954, p.260). It is here that a Movement ideology is first identified. The poetry of Philip Larkin is only briefly mentioned, along with the work of John Wain, Donald Davie, Kingsley Amis and Thom Gunn, but already a group personality is seen to exist. Stylistically, these writers share an avoidance of rhetoric, an austere tone and a colloquial idiom. The importance of Hartley's early review is that it acknowledges the political and cultural contours of a dominant literary tendency in post-war England. The 'liberalism' to which Hartley refers can be traced back to the kind of liberal idealism espoused by E.M. Forster in the early part of the twentieth century, but in Larkin's case it can only be fully understood in relation to the specific historical circumstances of English society after 1945. It is, as Hartley explains, 'A liberalism distrustful of too much fanaticism, austere and sceptical. A liberalism egalitarian and anti-aristocratic. A liberalism profoundly opposed to fashion in the metropolitan sense of the word . . .' (Hartley, 1954, p.260). This remains one of the best descriptions of Movement ideology, and it will be argued later that the shaping and development of Larkin's poetry is best understood within this context of English liberalism.

Hartley's confident remark that 'we are now in the presence of the only considerable movement in English poetry since the Thirties' (Hartley, 1954, p.261) is echoed in the title of a later *Spectator* article, 'In the Movement', by its editor J. D. Scott. Scott agrees that 'the English literary scene' has not been transformed in such a way since the 1930s, and contrasts the social, political and moral consciousness of that age with the seeming disengagement of the 1950s. Once again, the Movement is defined in terms of a lost idealism and in terms of a vigilant readjustment to an unsettled post-war England: 'The Movement, as well as being anti-phoney, is anti-wet; sceptical, robust, ironic, prepared to be as comfortable as possible in a wicked, commercial, threatened world which doesn't look, anyway, as if it's going to be changed much by a couple of handfuls of young English writers' (Scott, 1954, p.400).

It was the appearance of Larkin's poetry in several anthologies of the 1950s which gave further impetus to the idea of his collaboration with a movement in English poetry. The editors of *Springtime: An Anthology of Young Poets and Writers* (1953) speak in narrowly technical terms of a poetry which is 'going through a period of consolidation and simplification ... of reaction against experiment for its own sake', and they further claim that their chosen contributors are 'poets of an analytical habit of mind, whose aim is to clarify, by stating plainly, typical complex situations' (Fraser and Fletcher, 1953, pp.7–10).

The same emphasis on 'honesty of thought and feeling and clarity of expression' can be found in D.J. Enright's introduction to *Poets of the 1950s: An Anthology of New English Verse*, but Enright is clearly alert to the cultural conditions that have prompted this kind of poetic response. Echoing the *Spectator* articles, Enright acknowledges 'a new spirit stirring in contemporary English poetry' (Enright, 1955, p.15). He presents his anthology *not* as the work of a movement, however, but as a selection of poems by individual writers, some of whom share common attitudes. Like the *Spectator*, he stresses the distinction between the political commitment that characterised the poetry of the 1930s and the desired neutrality of the 1950s. Enright offers little explanation for this seeming retreat from political commitment, but his introduction nevertheless registers the disenchantment and general uncertainty of a post-war generation of writers.

The liberal humanist perspective identified by Hartley is given further clarification by Enright, who speaks of the need to 'resuscitate the idea of the dignity of the human individual' and of the way in which 'private responsibility' sometimes outweighs 'social responsibility' (Enright, 1955, pp.13–14). Despite Enright's disclaimers about a group identity, his poets seem to share a common set of values and assumptions: a vigilant individualism, a careful distancing of the private from the public, and a cautious avoidance of political commitment. Enright's poets are 'moderate': they exemplify 'chastened common sense' and they eschew obscurity 'because they find it unnecessary'. Enright demands from his contemporaries 'a fairly tough intelligence and an unwillingness to be deceived', and in doing so he suggests how closely the poetic ideals of the time were linked to the general scepticism that prevailed in post-war England (Enright, 1955, p.13). As we will discover later, it is no coincidence that in listing these 'virtues' Enright should allude to the title of Philip Larkin's volume of poems, *The Less Deceived*.

Had Enright's anthology been more widely distributed, the political and cultural significance of the Movement poets and their anxious relationship with the poetry of the 1930s might have been better understood by a later generation of readers and writers. As it happened, Enright's anthology probably received less attention than it deserved. Instead, the anthology which had the greatest impact and which was generally held to be most representative of the Movement was Robert Conquest's *New Lines* (1956). It was Conquest's introduction to the anthology which was largely responsible for encouraging the idea of a reaction against the excesses of 1940s romanticism. The poets of that decade, he argues, were 'encouraged to produce diffuse and sentimental verbiage', while the new generation holds to 'a rational structure and comprehensible language' (Conquest, 1956, pp.xiv–xv). Conquest shows little concern for the social and historical circumstances of post-war England and instead resorts to dubious cultural metaphors of sickness and health. The 1940s attitude to poetry induced a 'sort of corruption'; it led to 'a rapid collapse of public taste, from which we have not yet recovered'. The poetry of the 1950s, however, represents 'a new and healthy general standpoint . . . the restoration of a sound and fruitful attitude to poetry' (Conquest, 1956, pp.xii, xiv). Conquest's bombastic description of the new poetry is frequently cited as a manifesto for the Movement poets:

> If one had briefly to distinguish this poetry of the fifties from its predecessors, I believe the most important general point would be that it submits to no great systems of theoretical constructs nor agglomerations of unconscious commands. It is free from both mystical and logical compulsions and – like modern philosophy – is empirical in its attitude to all that comes. This reverence for the real person or event is, indeed, a part of the general intellectual ambience (in so far as that is not blind or retrogressive) of our time. (Conquest, 1956, pp.xiv–xv)

What Conquest seems to be saying here is that the poetry of the 1950s is characterised chiefly by its anti-dogmatic ideals, by a kind of aesthetic purity and philosophical detachment. There is an apparent disregard for the poetry of the 1930s in his jibe at 'theoretical constructs', but the principal target would seem to be Dylan Thomas. Conquest assumes that poetry can maintain a 'free' and neutral stance, and that 'empiricism' is, in itself, a guarantee of this neutrality. Even though Conquest defines the new poetry in negative terms – that is, largely in terms of what it is *not* – he cannot conceal the problems of a poetic theory that refuses to recognise its own 'theoretical constructs' and which condemns 'ideology' in the very moment of declaring its own interests and allegiances. A preoccupation with what is 'real' and 'honest' becomes a way of disguising those interests, of positing something 'authentic' against what is merely 'theoretical' and 'false'. These are the problems of a good deal of so-called Movement poetry and they were partly responsible for its eventual demise. The pose of neutrality and objectivity could not be sustained indefinitely; the tensions and conflicts of post-war England continued to disturb the equanimity of such poetry, and what began as something separate and detached was either made to look increasingly defensive and withdrawn or pushed towards a point of declaration. In the case of Philip Larkin, the fastidious restraint of *The Less Deceived* gradually gave way to a much more confrontational and openly polemical writing, especially in *High Windows*.

Conquest has since strongly denied the charge of having created a Movement manifesto, but what his anthology clearly shows, especially when read in conjunction with Enright's similar offering, is that unmistakable similarities of style and outlook existed among the rising generation of 1950s poets. This is certainly the opinion of Samuel Hynes, writing in the *Times Literary Supplement* in 1980: 'The poems resemble each other enough to suggest that a movement did in fact exist. And the prefaces that the contributors wrote for *Poets of the 1950s* confirm that view: these poets had a programme, they knew what they were for and against' (Hynes, 1980, p.699). A resemblance in attitudes and techniques is certainly evident in much of the Movement poetry that was anthologised in the 1950s and 1960s, and it is useful to compare such poems as Larkin's 'Deceptions' and Amis's 'Alternatives', or Davie's 'A Christening' and Larkin's 'The Whitsun Weddings'. The use of wit and irony is a prominent feature, and this often produces a poetry that seems defensive and guarded. While much of this poetry strives for clarity and intelligibility, it can at times appear tame and trivial. As critics have pointed out, the prevailing tone is urbane and academic. Many of the poems are too neatly prescriptive and look like pieces of versified literary criticism. Some of the titles provide an indication of a 'bookish' or 'middlebrow' attitude: Kingsley Amis's 'A Bookshop Idyll', D.J. Enright's 'The Verb to Think', Donald Davie's 'Rejoinder to a Critic' and 'Too Late for Satire', and John Wain's 'Reason for not Writing Nature Poetry' and 'Poem Without a Main Verb'. One of the shortcomings of Movement poetry is its tendency to make a virtue out of the civilised sensibility, to value intellectual detachment and 'urbanity' above all else. This cool, ironic aloofness can be mildly shocking, as in Amis's 'Shitty', but more often than not it leads to a shallow denial of human potential for change and development, as in Davie's 'A Christening', with its deeply cynical line: 'What we do best is breed'. Perhaps the most significant 'manifesto' within Movement poetry is Davie's 'Remembering the Thirties', which in many ways epitomises the cautious outlook of the Cold War years in its declaration that 'A neutral tone is nowadays preferred'. What the poem demonstrates most forcefully, however, is that the example of Auden and his contemporaries continued to have a powerful impression upon the post-war generation of writers and could never be simply forgotten.

One of the earliest appraisals of Movement poetry can be found in *Rule and Energy* by John Press. Although Press gives little credence to the publicity surrounding the Movement in the mid 1950s, he nevertheless ventures a critique of its aims and achievements. The new poets 'advance no systematic theory of poetry and offer no rigid set of dogmatic beliefs', but it is possible, Press claims, to summarise the main characteristics of their work:

> They all display a cautious scepticism, favour an empirical attitude, speak in carefully measured accents, and examine a problem with an alert wariness . . . All of these poets, mistrusting or ignoring the legacy of the Romantics and aiming at colloquial ease, decorum, shapeliness, elegance, are trying to bring back into the currency of the language the precision, the snap, the gravity, the decisive, clinching finality which have been lost since the late Augustan age. (Press, 1963, pp.45–6)

Here, Press is referring not just to a reaction against the 'neo-Romanticism' of the 1940s but to the whole trend of English poetry since the early nineteenth century. The Movement poets, in this respect, are seen to represent a new 'classicism' in English poetry. Yet it is clear throughout *Rule and Energy* that this distrust of inflated rhetoric and large emotional gestures is only one aspect of a much broader post-war tendency. The most striking characteristic feature of English poetry in these years, as Press insists at the outset of the book, is 'the general retreat from direct comment on or involvement with any political or social doctrine'. This is particularly noticeable, he adds, 'if we contrast the verse of the past two decades with that of the nineteen thirties' (Press, 1963, p.5). What disturbs Press is the peculiar passivity of post-war poetry. He speculates that the establishment of the Welfare State may have mitigated some of the more glaring political and social injustices, but continues: '. . . it is absurd to pretend that in our affluent society a poet can find nothing to arouse his compassion or his savage indignation' (Press, 1963, p.11). The importance of this statement is that it very accurately identifies the 'neutral tone' of the new poetry and it seeks to explain it in terms of its historical context. In 1962, however, Philip Larkin had not yet published *The Whitsun Weddings* and Press was able to offer only a brief and tentative analysis of Larkin's work.

In 1980 Blake Morrison produced the first full-length study of the Movement, proposing that it was 'a literary group of considerable importance', as central to the 1950s as 'the Auden generation' was to the 1930s. Morrison asks a number of crucially revealing questions: 'Did the writers know each other? Is there any evidence of mutual admiration, mutual influence, or collaboration? Did the writers come from the same social background? Did they have similar political beliefs? Did they intend to write for the same kind of audience? Was there a common belief about the direction which contemporary literature should take?' (Morrison, 1980, pp.5–6). To all of these questions Morrison responds positively, and he goes on to argue decisively and persuasively that despite some obvious divisions and contradictions, 'for a time at least, there was considerable agreement and interaction, and that out of these was established a Movement consensus'. 'It is even possible', he suggests, 'to talk of a Movement "ideology" – an identifiable "line" on sex, religion, politics . . .' (Morrison, 1980, pp.6, 9). In addition, Morrison offers some illuminating contextual readings of Larkin's poetry (he considers *The Whitsun Weddings* as a Movement collection) and further demonstrates how Larkin 'continued to defend and develop principles central to the Movement programme' (Morrison, 1980, p.8).

The great strength of Morrison's book lies in its acute analysis of class and culture in the post-war years. What was especially significant, Morrison believes, is that Movement writers were identified by their contemporaries with a spirit of change in post-war British society and were thought to be representative of shifts in power and social structure. They were seen, that is, to have benefited from the new opportunities made available to the lower-middle and working classes and were therefore regarded by some members of the ruling class as a threat to the old order. Evelyn Waugh spoke of 'a new wave of philistinism with which we are threatened by these grim young people coming off the assembly lines in their hundreds every year and finding employment as critics, even as poets and novelists', while Somerset Maugham callously dismissed the same people as 'scum':

> They do not go to university to acquire culture, but to get a job, and when they have got one, scamp it. They have no manners, and are woefully unable to deal with any social predicament. Their idea of a celebration is to go to a public house and drink six beers. They are mean, malicious, and envious. (Morrison, 1980, pp.58–9)

Morrison, however, finds that the Movement writers were very far from rebellious; they were, in many ways, meekly submissive and often given to compromise and conservatism:

> What emerges in the work of the Movement, then, is an uneasy combination of class-consciousness and acceptance of class division; an acute awareness of privilege, but an eventual submission to the structure which makes it possible ... As spokesmen for the new self-proclaimed lower-middle-class intelligentsia, the Movement was forced into an ambivalent position; on the one hand opposed to the 'old order'; on the other hand indebted to, and respectful towards, its institutions. (Morrison, 1980, pp.74–5)

Morrison attributes this ambivalence to the fact that most of the Movement poets were scholarship boys in centres of learning still largely dominated by the upper-middle class and therefore subject to pressures to understate social difference. Larkin himself refers to this process in the introduction to his novel *Jill*, where he admits that in Oxford in 1940 'our impulse was still to minimize social differences rather than exaggerate them' (Larkin, 1983, p.17). Furthermore, the influence of thinkers like F.R. Leavis, especially in such subjects as English, undoubtedly helped to promote the kind of conformity and spirit of national unity that Morrison detects.

Despite its mood of dissent and its anti-establishment attitude, the Movement offered only 'a token rebellion', and did not attempt to change the prevailing social structure. The ambivalence of Movement politics becomes particularly evident in the immediate context of the post-war years and manifests itself in a wavering liberal attitude towards the changing balance of power in the new society. The Movement poets were clearly influenced by the democratic idealism that accompanied the Labour victory of 1945, however short-lived that spirit of optimism might have been, and yet most of them were distrustful of egalitarian political ideals and remained deeply suspicious of radical change.

Given this ambivalence in politics, it is not surprising to discover in the work of Movement writers a sense of nostalgia and regret in the face of Britain's inevitable decline as a world power. Blake Morrison diagnoses the Movement predicament very astutely and shows how it operates in the poetry. Donald Davie's poem 'The Garden Party', for instance, seems at first sight to be severely critical of both class division and capitalism, yet the speaker of the poem has benefited too well from the current social structure to wish to change it. The poem ends in compromise, seeming to offer a critique of existing social arrangements but carefully maintaining a sense of distance and neutrality. The Movement, then, for all its initial anti-establishment fervour, proved to be politically inoffensive. In contrast to the poets of the 1930s, many of whom were upper-middle-class political activists, the poets of the 1950s were lower-middle class and politically neutral.

What is particularly impressive about Morrison's thesis is that it demonstrates how the Movement's social and political ambivalence extends into the formal and structural texture of the poetry in terms of hesitations, qualifications and conversational asides. In fact the whole sense of an audience in Movement poetry, Morrison argues, is shaped by questions of socio-political identity, especially by the difficulty of appealing to an academic élite and at the same time being responsible to the general public in a modern democracy. Morrison explains the alleged 'anti-romanticism' of the Movement not as a narrow literary response to the work of Dylan Thomas but as a careful strategy in a Britain more intent on pursuing communal and egalitarian ideals than it had been before the Second World War. In the new Welfare State democracy this amounted to an admission that the poet was not 'a mystic or visionary removed from society' but a 'responsible citizen responsibly employed' (Morrison, 1980, p.178).

Further confirmation of the Movement's political caution can be found in Robert Hewison's well-documented account of the post-war years, *In Anger: Culture in the Cold War 1945–60* (1981). Rather comically, Hewison reminds us that 'the Movement did not exist' (it was, he believes, an effective piece of stage management), but he himself can hardly avoid using the label (Hewison, 1981, p.86). His essential point is that the attitudes of the Movement poets reflect the restrictive conditions of the Cold War. In other words, the neutrality, caution and self-limitation of these writers belong to the mood of fear and suspicion created by the continuing opposition among the military and diplomatic forces of East and West after 1945:

> The Cold War tended to freeze public attitudes, and counselled silence about private ones. It recommended a guarded private life, in which only small gestures were possible, gestures chiefly about the difficulty of making a gesture. Hence the concern of the Movement poets with the problems of perception and expression. (Hewison, 1981, p.122)

It should be clear that *literary* history alone does not provide an adequate explanation for what prompted the Movement and determined the kind of poetry it stood for. A reaction against Dylan Thomas is of little significance unless it is placed in a post-war context where heightened rhetoric and inflated emotion were likely to be regarded with suspicion. The Movement cannot be abstracted from the social and political history of those post-war years. It should be clear, too, that the correct measure of the aims and achievements of Movement poetry is to be found not just in the romantic poetry of the 1940s (against which it appears cool and rational) but in the socialist writings of the 1930s (against which it appears neutral and defensive).

It will be argued later that an understanding of the intellectual formation outlined above is an essential prerequisite for an alert and responsible reading of Philip Larkin's poetry. The early poetry, in particular, clearly coincides with the Movement ideology described in this chapter, especially in its struggle for neutral ground. The creation of a self-effacing, 'modest' discourse and a self-deprecating, ironic persona is immediately apparent in the poems of *The Less Deceived*; so too is a distrust of large, idealistic gestures and a preference for English provincial settings over those of 'abroad'. Along with the anti-metropolitan and anti-cosmopolitan instincts in Larkin's poetry, there is a sedulous avoidance of any direct treatment of recent history. This does not mean, however, that the poems themselves somehow 'transcend' history. Blake Morrison has shown how well a poem like 'Church Going' fits the Movement 'programme' by carefully balancing agnostic dissent with a susceptibility to tradition and belief; it appears to be both reverent and irreverent. In keeping with Movement preferences, the poem has a traditional iambic structure and a lucid, rational argument; its speaker is presented as an ordinary, fallible and clumsy individual. It is a poem which testifies to the persistence of both the English church and an English poetic tradition (Morrison, 1980, pp.225–37).

There are, of course, important ways in which Larkin's poetry departs from Movement principles, and these tendencies were evident even before the Movement dissolved into divergent lines. Morrison claims that Larkin is much more astute than his peers in his sense of audience and perhaps more sympathetically attuned to the Romantic influences that Movement poetry professed to scorn. Samuel Hynes in reviewing Morrison's book claims that Larkin's work is more 'expansive' and more 'wide-ranging' than that of other Movement poets (Hynes, 1980, p.699). Many critics are convinced that Larkin is a 'better' poet than Amis, Wain, Enright and Davie without being entirely sure why. We ought to confront issues of this kind as openly as possible and be prepared to discuss and debate what we 'value' in poetry. While placing Larkin's poetry firmly in the context of post-war England and its attendant hopes and fears, this particular study will also be concerned with the extent to which that poetry operates *beyond* the Movement consensus. Implicit in its argument is a belief that Larkin's poetry, in contrast with the work of other 'Movement' writers, not only exemplifies a deeper imaginative apprehension of social experience and its contradictions, but that it exhibits a far greater range of formal and stylistic devices and a more profound sense of the linguistic and aesthetic possibilities of modern colloquial English.

Gentility in English Poetry

In 1963 Robert Conquest published a second anthology of contemporary poetry, *New Lines II*, in which he once again paid tribute to the persistence and variety of 'the central current of English verse'. Modernist innovations such as might be found in the poetry of Ezra Pound were, for Conquest, little more than 'peripheral additions to the main tradition of English poetry'. Acknowledging the work of Philip Larkin as an essential continuation of this tradition, Conquest continued in a vein of strident anti-modernism:

> One even comes across the impudent assertion that English poets were unaware of the existence of the darker elements in the human personality, and of large-scale suffering, until psychoanalysts and world wars drew attention to them, and this is compounded with transparently spurious logic, by the notion that the way to cope with these forces is to abandon sanity and hope. (Conquest, 1963, pp.xiii–xiv)

Without being explicit about the matter, Conquest was responding to a rival anthology, *The New Poetry* (1962), in which Alfred Alvarez had strongly criticised the work of the Movement (and Larkin in particular) for failing to deal with the full range of human experience. The obvious irritation in Conquest's rejoinder is an indication of the profound impact that Alvarez had made on contemporary literary criticism. By throwing 'tradition' and 'experiment' into sharp relief, *The New Poetry* undoubtedly stimulated one of the liveliest debates in the history of twentieth-century poetry. Twenty years later, Andrew Motion and Blake Morrison, the editors of *The Penguin Book of Contemporary British Poetry*, were among those still trying to counteract its influence. Significantly, both editors have strong professional interests in Larkin and the Movement.

To some extent the Alvarez approach had been anticipated by the editors of an earlier anthology, *Mavericks* (1957), also designed to restrict the monopoly of the Movement. Dannie Abse complained that the Movement attitude was 'fundamentally anti-poetic . . . it is as if they're afraid of the mystery conversing with the mystery'. Howard Sergeant agreed that the Movement showed a 'lack of motivating impulse' and had 'little of particular urgency or import-ance to say' (Sergeant and Abse, 1957, pp.9, 12). 'Urgency' was to become a key word in the critical vocabulary of Alvarez and an indication of what was essentially lacking in Movement poetry.

The most formidable attack on Larkin and the Movement prior to Alvarez, however, was launched by Charles Tomlinson in a review of the *New Lines* anthology titled 'The Middlebrow Muse' (1957). After expressing his distaste for Larkin's 'intense parochialism', Tomlinson went on to make more general assertions about the 'stale feeling of ordinariness, of second-hand responses' which typified the work of the *New Lines* poets:

> They show a singular want of vital awareness of the continuum outside themselves, of the mystery bodied over against them in the created universe, which they fail to experience with any degree of sharpness or to embody with any instress or sensuous depth . . . They seldom for a moment escape beyond the suburban mental ratio which they impose on experience. (Tomlinson, 1957, p.215)

'Mystery' and 'experience' are the tokens by which Tomlinson defines the restrictions and limitations of Movement poetry. In short, the Movement represents 'not so much a creative re-direction as a total failure of nerve' (Tomlinson, 1957, p.215). Whereas Blake Morrison understands 'failure of nerve' in terms of the specific difficulties experienced by certain writers in confronting political and cultural issues, Tomlinson applies the phrase in a general way to suggest a fundamental lack of vision. Tomlinson repeated this criticism in 'Poetry Today', a contribution to *The Pelican Guide to English Literature: The Modern Age* (1973). Movement poetry, he claimed, was supposed to be 'empirical in its attitude to all that comes'. 'But how much', he asked, 'was allowed to come before the poet?' What Tomlinson objects to in Larkin's poetry is a 'wry and sometimes tenderly nursed sense of defeat', a melancholy introspec-tion that seems to possess a peculiarly English appeal:

> Larkin's narrowness suits the English perfectly. They recognize their own abysmal urban landscapes, skilfully caught with just a

whiff of English films *circa* 1950. The stepped-down version of human possibilities ... the joke that hesitates just on this side of nihilism, are national vices. (Tomlinson, 1973, pp.471, 478–9)

All the terms of a particular and familiar criticism of Larkin's poetry are established here: the recognition of a certain 'skill', but a more emphatic disdain for the poet's defeatism, narrowness, parochialism and pessimism. Subsequent critics have challenged these terms and have tried to argue that the poetry reveals a more 'affirmative' view of human existence. One might go further and question the alternative poetic experience which Tomlinson proposes in such abstruse language as 'the continuum outside themselves ... the mystery bodied over against them in the created universe'. Such an argument implies a wilful abnegation of the 'social' in favour of the 'psychological'. Tomlinson is justified, perhaps, in tilting at the 'middlebrow muse' that seems to inform the poetry, but there is no attempt to understand that 'middlebrow' quality in terms of the changing nature of authorship and readership in the post-war years.

A similar set of preferences can be found in the introduction to *The New Poetry* by Alfred Alvarez. Where Tomlinson berates 'parochialism' and summons 'vital awareness', Alvarez dispenses with 'gentility' and calls for 'urgency'. To support his argument, Alvarez quotes Thomas Hardy's remark to Robert Graves: 'All we can do is to write on the old themes in the old styles, but try to do a little better than those who went before us' (Alvarez, 1966, p.21). Since about 1930, he argues, modern English poetry has been shaped by a series of 'negative feed-backs' restraining any progressive or experimental tendency. First, he claims, the poets of the 1930s reacted against the writers of the 1920s, because the immediate political situation demanded something other than 'difficult', 'inward' or 'experimental' poetry. Second, the followers of Dylan Thomas in the 1940s reacted against the dry social observation of W.H. Auden and his generation by writing a more romantic, stylised kind of verse. Third, there was a reaction against the 'wild, loose emotion' of the 1940s by the Movement. 'The pieties of the Movement', Alvarez says, were 'as predictable as the politics of the thirties poets'. Referring generally to the work of Larkin and his contemporaries, Alvarez states: 'It was, in short, academic-administrative verse, knowledgeable, efficient, polished, and, in its quiet way, even intelligent' (Alvarez, 1966, pp.24–5). We might well ask if poetic 'influence' is as mechanical and deliberate as Alvarez suggests, and we might wish to challenge his use of the word 'negative'. In what sense were these 'feed-backs' *designed*? Was Thomas Hardy's influence on modern poetry an entirely negative one, and did nothing positive emerge from the various 'feed-backs' that Alvarez observes in the history of twentieth-century poetry? While expressing doubts and reservations about its fundamental assertions, it is still possible to recognise 'Beyond the Gentility Principle' as an outstanding piece of provocative and polemical writing. Like all successful anthologies, *The New Poetry* presents its argument with force and clarity.

It is important to note what position Larkin occupies within the third negative feed-back described in *The New Poetry*. Alvarez chooses the lines 'Hatless, I take off / My cycle-clips in awkward reverence' (from 'Church Going') and proceeds to analyse them in the terms established in his thesis:

> This, in concentrated form, is the image of the post-war Welfare State Englishman: shabby and not concerned with his appearance; poor – he has a bike, not a car; gauche but full of agnostic piety; underfed, underpaid, overtaxed, hopeless, bored, wry. This is the third negative feed-back: an attempt to show that the poet is not a strange creature inspired; on the contrary, he is just like the man next door – in fact, he probably *is* the man next door. (Alvarez, 1966, pp.24–5)

Once again it is necessary to press the question: why should such ordinariness be construed as 'negative'? It might also be worth asking if Alvarez makes any distinction between 'the poet' and 'the persona' of the depressed observer who frequently inhabits Larkin's poetry. The persona of 'Church Going' is perhaps more 'modern' in sensibility than Alvarez allows. Charles Tomlinson had at least acknowledged Larkin's 'ironic self-deprecating vein' and its similarities with the work of Jules Laforgue (the prominent influence behind T.S. Eliot's J. Alfred Prufrock). There is, nevertheless, a great deal of validity in Alvarez's overall assessment of Movement poetry, especially in his definition of gentility. 'Gentility', he argues, is 'a belief that life is always more or less orderly, people always more or less polite, their emotions and habits more or less decent and more or less controllable; that God, in short, is more or less good' (Alvarez, 1966, p.25). As we will see later, it is not too difficult to discover poems by Larkin which firmly contradict these 'genteel' assumptions. The real weakness of the Alvarez thesis, however, lies in what he advocates as the prevailing quality of 'the new poetry': it amounts, in short, to 'urgency'.

What poetry needs, in Alvarez's estimation, is 'a new seriousness', a recognition of the forces of evil and disintegration which have emerged from two world wars, the concentration camps and the threat of nuclear war. The growing need to explore and understand these 'forces' has accompanied modern developments in psychology and psychoanalysis. In poetry, such forces are notably present in the work of American writers such as Robert Lowell, John Berryman, Sylvia Plath and Anne Sexton, who were able to produce 'poetry of immense skill and intelligence which coped openly with the quick of their experience, experience sometimes on the edge of disintegration and breakdown' (Alvarez, 1966, pp.28–9). It is necessary at once to correct the implication that Larkin, by contrast, is a poet who blithely ignores those fears and desires that impinge upon everyday existence and whose work has only a limited psychological reference. Furthermore, it becomes evident that Alvarez can sustain his argument only by privileging the individual psyche over the broader social formation, with the consequence that he appears to value a poetry that is 'urgently personal' over a poetry that is socially and politically responsive. There is a very obvious danger in continually abstracting the individual psyche from the complex historical and political determinants of twentieth-century culture. It is deeply worrying, for instance, to find Alvarez attributing what he regards as the destruction of 'the old standards of civilization' to shifts in libido.

Alvarez's preference for a poetry that is intensely 'psychological' is evident in his discussion of Larkin's 'At Grass' and Ted Hughes's 'A Dream of Horses'. It might be argued that the choice of two poems which just happen to include horses is a rather spurious, even facile, critical procedure, but the results are nevertheless interesting. Larkin's poem is 'more skilful but less urgent' than 'A Dream of Horses'; it is 'elegant and unpretentious and rather beautiful in its gentle way', but Hughes's poem is 'unquestionably *about* something; it is a serious attempt to re-create and so clarify ... a powerful complex of emotions and sensations'. Alvarez's tendency to privilege 'psychology' over everything else is evident in his implication that

Larkin's poem is not really *about* anything in particular; Larkin's horses are '*social* creatures' (his italics) while Hughes's horses 'reach back, as in a dream, into a nexus of fear and sensation. Their brute world is part physical, part state of mind' (Alvarez, 1962, pp.30–1). The 'social' is accordingly downgraded in favour of primitive mystification.

'Gentility' and 'urgency' are useful descriptive terms, but as categories by which to judge and evaluate the entire scope of post-war poetry they are arbitrary and invalid. The Alvarez thesis is stimulating and provocative but is ultimately misleading. What Alvarez fails to perceive is that those apparent 'limitations' which he associates with Movement poetry are as much a symptom of wartime England as the 'urgent' psychological pressures which he regards as a more authentic indication of the state of modern culture. As Andrew Crozier has argued, a very different thesis can be constructed if the critical starting point is the similarity rather than the difference between the two poems by Larkin and Hughes: 'Both poems are allegories of an absent fullness of being . . . What differentiates the poems is their approach to the nostalgia of diminished being . . . Neither poet questions the sources or conditions of such feelings, but takes them for granted' (Crozier, 1983, pp.217–18). For Crozier, it matters little whether one poem is more overtly psychological than the other; what is more important is that both are inscribed with a sense of loss and diminishment which has its specific origins in the material conditions of post-war England.

Crozier argues further that while Alvarez's notion of gentility and Tomlinson's 'suburban mental ratio' are roughly identical, Tomlinson is more radical in his criticism of Larkin and the Movement. Alvarez, he claims, is actually in broad agreement with Conquest about 'the proper mode of discourse of poetry'. Both the *New Lines* poetry and the 'confessional' work admired by Alvarez rely on lyric forms, often dramatic in presentation, and both employ elaborate figurative devices (such as horses) to effect a link between speaker and object. Crozier's article offers a powerfully sustained critique of the whole Movement ethos in post-war poetry and should be regarded as a vital contribution to this particular debate.

Allowing for the subtle distinctions proposed by Crozier, it would seem that most of the adverse reaction to Larkin's work has followed the broad line of criticism initiated by Tomlinson and Alvarez. In the United States, M.L. Rosenthal argued in *The Modern Poets* that

Larkin's work was marred by a petty bitterness: 'the sullenness of a man who finds squalor in his own spirit and fears to liberate himself from it' (Rosenthal, 1965, p.222). Two years later he repeated his objections in *The New Poets*, agreeing with Alvarez that 'there is little in Larkin to resemble the large risks that Hughes takes' (Rosenthal, 1967, p.234). Colin Falck was also among those who complained that 'there are no epiphanies' in Larkin's poetry, no high points of 'beauty or truth or love' (Falck, 1968, p.109). Falck concedes that the 'ordinariness' of Larkin's work grants it 'a certain kind of humanity', but the poet, he thinks, should transform rather than merely accept the 'ordinary' world and so provide a more uplifting vision for his readers. Falck's desire for a more heightened poetic response, however, leads him towards a dangerous and irresponsible assumption: 'In rejecting Larkin's particular brand of "humanism" I may seem to be asking for the kind of "right wing" violence to which D.H. Lawrence was sometimes led. I think perhaps I am' (Falck, 1968, p.110). The assumption is that the democratic impulse in post-war England has fostered a mediocre poetry and that the best art is the product of the privileged few within a more hierarchical and authoritarian society. The same suspect notion lies behind Charles Tomlinson's complaint in 'The Middlebrow Muse' that moderate talents have managed to find a cosy corner in 'our watered-down democratic culture' (Tomlinson, 1957, p.216).

Donald Davie takes issue with both Falck and Tomlinson in his 'Landscapes of Larkin', asserting that Larkin, unlike Lawrence, 'agrees to tolerate the intolerable for the sake of human solidarity'. In acknowledging Larkin's humanism, however, Davie does not substantially alter the terms of the argument and sometimes makes Larkin sound extremely dull. In fact, Davie's attempt to justify a poetry of 'lowered sights and patiently diminished expectations' has come to be regarded as one of the most negative responses to Larkin's work (Davie, 1973, pp.69–71). In the process, Davie's very significant remarks about the nature of Larkin's 'humanism' and the democratic basis of his writing have been overlooked. Part of Davie's endeavour is directed towards a revaluation of the Hardy tradition that Alvarez had sought to undermine. Larkin is seen as 'a very Hardyesque poet' with a thoroughly English soul – 'the England in his poems is the England we have inhabited' (Davie, 1973, p.64). Unfortunately, Davie is a little too glib in his idea of what constitutes 'Englishness' and too readily assumes that Larkin effectively speaks for all England and for all social classes. His use of the collective pronoun in the quoted phrase is much too casual.

Calvin Bedient restates many of the familiar claims about Larkin's limited subject matter but his assessment of the poetry is positive and appreciative. For Bedient, Larkin is 'unillusioned, with a metaphysical zero in his bones', and his poetry exemplifies 'the withering of the ideal, of romance, of possibility, that characterizes post-war thought'. From this perspective there is a degree of inevitability about Larkin's subject matter; what matters is Larkin's technique in responding to the diminished possibilities of his time. Echoing Tomlinson's remarks about the nihilistic tendencies in Larkin's poetry, Bedient emphasises that 'Larkin's distinction from other nihilists lies in his domestication of the void: he has simply taken nullity for granted, found it as banal as the worn places in linoleum' (Bedient, 1974, pp.70–1). The saving grace of the poetry is the style with which it confronts a pervasive sense of emptiness. Bedient praises 'the combined plea and protest' of Larkin's linguistic constructions, with their 'exemplary inner necessity, their perfection' (Bedient, 1974, p.80). The importance of Bedient's essay is that it suggests how the formal structure of Larkin's work might be understood in terms of its post-war intellectual context.

For David Holbrook, writing about Larkin in *Lost Bearings in English Poetry*, the numbness and caution identified by other critics are not so much symptoms of post-war culture as facets of the poet's individual psychology. In a heavily moralistic way, Larkin is seen to be deficient in human kindness; lacking even the 'solidarity' claimed for him by Donald Davie. In the final stanza of 'The Whitsun Weddings', Holloway finds the poet attempting 'to open his heart to others, or about others', but '. . . the heart is dead'. 'The Whitsun Weddings', he argues, 'not only displays the educated writer cut off from the people, but a man whose perceptions, curiosities and versifications cannot be creative, cannot find and communicate "the power that being changed can give" even though he knows he should' (Holbrook, 1977, pp.168, 174). There is undoubtedly some justification in Holbrook's perception of the writer 'cut off from the people', but there is no attempt to understand this division in class or cultural terms; instead, it is judged as a peculiarity of individual behaviour. Holbrook is content to see the speaker of the poem simply as 'Larkin' and accordingly shows a lamentable deficiency in responding to the poetry as structure and discourse. There are shades of Alvarez in the claim that Larkin's work possesses 'a certain kind of linguistic genteel quality', but the principal characteristic of Holbrook's criticism is its hyperactive moralising.

One of the most formidable replies to the negative criticism of Alvarez and others can be found in J.R. Watson's stimulating essay, 'The Other Larkin'. Watson detects in the Alvarez argument 'a disproportionate concentration on the surface properties of the poet and his work, and a disinclination to admit that there is anything deeper or more complex'. Claiming that critics have wrongly taken Larkin's dramatic personae at face value, Watson disputes the idea that the outlook of the poems is typified by 'a limiting and debilitating gentility' (Watson, 1975, p.347). What frequently occurs in Larkin's poems is a progression 'from a poise, or a pose, to an exposure or an epiphany'. Where Falck insists that 'there are no epiphanies', Watson argues to the contrary that 'Larkin's poetry celebrates the unexpressed, deeply felt longings for sacred time and sacred space' (Watson, 1975, pp.348, 354). The suggestion that the poetry embodies 'forgotten patterns of belief and ritual' is well illustrated by 'The Whitsun Weddings'. The most important aspect of 'The Other Larkin' is its emphasis on the ways in which Christianity 'seeks to accommodate itself to a world in which the old patterns of belief have disappeared' (Watson, 1975, pp.350, 360). It has since become fashionable to emphasise the 'transcendent' element in Larkin's poetry as a way of contesting the rather dull and unexciting terms in which the early Larkin criticism was posited. What has been lost in the meantime is a concern for the secular or 'desacralized' context in which Larkin's poetry was written and in which it continues to be read.

Thematic Approaches

A familiar list of thematic interests and concerns appears in Larkin criticism with wearying regularity. Time, death, chance and choice: these are the very stuff of Larkin's poetry, we are told. Larkin's detractors point to the narrowness of this range of themes, while admirers praise his distinctive treatment of these fundamentally poetic concerns. Anthony Thwaite is among those who define Larkin's greatness as a writer according to his handling of a traditional and perennial subject matter: 'His themes – love, change, disenchantment, the mystery and inexplicableness of the past's survival and death's finality – are unshakably major' (Thwaite, 1970, p.54). John Wain echoes these sentiments when he writes of Larkin that 'we shall hardly get a grip on his poetry unless we succeed in bringing into relief its principal themes'. 'One of these', he tells us, is 'the act of choosing' and another is 'the effect of time in individual lives' (Wain, 1976, pp.98, 100). For both critics it would seem that history – whether as 'the past' or as 'time' – is to be regarded as just one more theme. The unfortunate effect of this view of history as subject matter is its tendency to ignore the extent to which Larkin's poetry is itself a product of history. Thematic criticism approaches the ideas of an author or text in terms of 'universal relevance', thereby giving little consideration to the often complex relationships between 'ideas' and particular phases of social and cultural change. Thematic criticism, then, not only leads to a reductive reading of the poems by concentrating on a monotonous range of topics, it also responds to ideas in a patently unhistorical way.

A persistent claim in thematic criticism is that 'time' in Larkin's poetry is not only 'inexplicable' but also 'unchangeable'. In an early essay, C.B. Cox states that among Larkin's 'best' poems are 'many which deal simply with universal themes of time, suffering and death'. Discussing 'Next, Please', he suggests that 'Illusion is interwoven with all our thinking, for we can never escape from the inadequacy of the present' (Cox, 1959, pp.15–16). Why the present should be 'inadequate' or why such an attitude should be registered so forcefully in the poem is never considered. Cox's intention is to recognise Larkin as one of the most 'important' poets of the 1950s, and he is therefore at pains to dissociate Larkin from the other writers who came to maturity during the 1939–45 war and who have since 'succumbed to uncertainty or pessimism' (Cox, 1959, p.14). He continues his discussion of 'Next, Please' by explaining that Larkin 'does not rebel because failure seems to him one of the unchangeable facts of life. We cannot alter these facts of our experience' (Cox, 1959, p.15). What is disturbing here is that the attitude of resignation that the poem dramatises is simply taken for granted and elevated into a general principle. That attitude is neither held up for critical inspection nor understood in relation to its times. In other words, the adopted critical stance seems to replicate and endorse the passivity and conformity that the poem is ostensibly concerned with.

Thematic criticism of this kind is usually based on the assumption that there is a fundamental 'human condition' (witness 'these facts of our experience') which is essentially unchanging, just as the themes of great poetry are timeless and universal. Alan Brownjohn begins his 1975 British Council monograph by outlining Larkin's predominant themes and goes on to discuss the poet's 'particular kind of compassionate despair at the human condition' (Brownjohn, 1975, p.15). 'Faith Healing', the poem under discussion, depicts a group of elderly people whose vulnerability is exploited by an American evangelical preacher. Blake Morrison suggests that 'Faith Healing' was prompted by Billy Graham's visits to England in the 1950s (Morrison, 1980, p.223). What is 'particular' about the poem, then, is its context and not just its outlook; it is not so much a poem about 'the human condition' as about the nature of belief and disbelief in a 'particular' phase of twentieth-century culture. The poem recognises that 'In everyone there sleeps a sense of life lived according to love', but the attitudes and values which inform such a statement and give it prominence within the poem are those of a troubled post-war agnostic sensibility. As with 'Church Going', the punning title refers not so much to a static condition as to an active cultural and theological *process*.

In the final paragraph of his study Brownjohn tells us that Larkin has 'looked for his values to the past and the customs deriving from it, seeing in the present only the irreversible recession of all innocence, worth and sweetness from human living, and in the future nothing more than a process of unbearable decline and death . . .'. Nevertheless, he continues, Larkin has 'made out of this bitter, unalterable situation a poetry that is indisputably modern in its content and its cadences' (Brownjohn, 1975, p.32). Brownjohn initially distances himself from the attitudes implicit in the poems but seems lulled into a passive acceptance of the world view that they represent. Consequently he fails to inspect these attitudes with sufficient critical detachment and gives little consideration to what might have prompted them. More worrying is his tendency to regard such a dismal and depressing state of affairs as 'unalterable'. Such poems as 'Going, Going' or 'Homage to a Government' suggest, to the contrary, that change of one kind or another is entirely possible and is often dependent on alternative modes of government and social structure. To speak of the essential concerns of Larkin's poetry as 'unalterable' is to reproduce their most pessimistic and fatalistic tendencies without regard for the trenchant ironies and rhetorical provocations which they frequently display. Brownjohn's final sentence acknowledges the way in which Larkin's poetry catches 'the experience of common men in the twentieth century', which once again implies that there is a single 'human condition' and consequently fails to do justice to the complex ways in which Larkin's poetry registers a sense of class and cultural differences in post-war England.

A concentration on the thematic aspects of literary texts has been encouraged by the ideas and techniques of *practical criticism* (or *new criticism* in the United States). Practical criticism was a method developed by I.A. Richards in a book of that title (1929), and until recently it dominated the teaching of English literature in secondary and higher education. The publication of Larkin's poems coincided significantly with the resurgence of practical criticism after the Second World War and selections from *The Less Deceived* and *The Whitsun Weddings* were frequently chosen as suitable exercises. In *Modern Poetry: Studies in Practical Criticism* (1963) C.B. Cox and A.E. Dyson acknowledge the cultural beliefs and ideals that informed practical criticism when they announce that the new poets 'express much compassion for the ordinary human condition, and through their art demonstrate that the mind can still impose some order on the chaotic experience of twentieth-century living'. Philip Larkin is of special relevance here because his poetry 'proves that order can be created in small areas of personal relationships' (Cox and Dyson, 1963, pp.30–1). In application, practical criticism claims to be neutral and disinterested in its view of the world, and yet its preoccupation with 'order' in the modern world clearly suggests an important social and political purpose.

Central to practical criticism is the conviction that 'analysis of themes should go side by side with an examination of technique' (Cox and Dyson, 1963, p.22). For this reason, practical criticism is often regarded as being largely *formalist* in its approach. Cox and Dyson discourage students from offering 'a simple cliché-ridden summary of attitudes to love or death or God', and suggest instead that they should try to find words which do justice to 'the honest impression' which they have received from the text (Cox and Dyson, 1963, p.22). The first recommendation is admirable but the second seems unnecessarily prescriptive about the scope of enquiry and about the kind of knowledge that texts can afford. The consequences of such a criticism are evident in the editors' sample reading of Larkin's 'At Grass', a poem which is thought to remind its readers of 'the pathos of old age and the swift passing of time' and which 'celebrates the mystery of the human lot' (Cox and Dyson, 1963, pp.138–9). In a very impressive and informative way, the article comments upon the technical achievements of the poem, including its imagery, metre, rhythm and syntax, but the possible 'meanings' of the poem are heavily generalised. At one point we are told, with unusual candour, that the final stanza of the poem demonstrates 'how the impositions of society, which forces purposes and categories upon us, are taken away'. What these impositions are and how, in human terms, they might be 'taken away' are not explained. The article moves sombrely on to consider the inevitability of the horses' fate: 'As they are taken back to the stables, it is as if, as with all men, they are submitting to death' (Cox and Dyson, 1963, pp.140–1).

A more insistently formalist reading of the poetry can be found in Philip Hobsbaum's essay, 'Larkin's Singing Line'. Commenting on the final stanza of 'At Grass', Hobsbaum points to the syntactic inversion of the closing line, the half-rhymes of 'home' and 'come', and the subtle inner pararhyme of 'groom'. The effect, he says, is 'to feel the voice hush and the imagery become subdued'. The inverted syntax is 'part of the subdued and delaying echo of the verse. Both elements are part of an effect conveying the sense of evening and impending death'. We do not need to think too hard about what the poem means, since 'the conceptual content of a poem is usually slight, and not remarkable for its originality' (Hobsbaum, 1988, pp.285–6). What the critic needs, above all, is a good pair of ears. Such an attitude, of course, ensures that the critic is suitably 'subdued'. Nearly always, this kind of formalist criticism resorts to platitudes about the human condition; it cannot sustain its intense concentration on style and technique without some reference to ideas and meanings. So, predictably, we learn that 'Here' suggests 'the limitations imposed on us by mortal life which hurries us from one mode of living to another' and that the music of 'Church Going' conveys 'the isolation of contemporary man' (Hobsbaum, 1988, pp.288–9). The peculiar achievement of Hobsbaum's article lies in its combination of an acute sensitivity to the lyrical cadences of poetry with a seeming disregard for social and historical realities.

It is not surprising, in view of the widespread influence of practical criticism, that most book-length studies of Philip Larkin's poetry should employ the familiar model of thematic analysis and examination of technique. The earliest critical study, by David Timms, shows how aspects of meaning in poetry are 'enacted' by metrical effects. Discussing the third stanza of 'At Grass', Timms tells us:

> The lines describe the scene, but the change in metre makes us hear and see it. Where the other stanzas are written in iambic pentameters, reversals of feet in this third stanza turn the first halves of these three lines into rocking choriambics, enacting the horses' gallop. (Timms, 1973, p.74)

'At Grass' is, in fact, written in iambic tetrameter, *not* iambic pentameter. Like Cox and Dyson, Timms believes that the poem 'celebrates withdrawal from the insistent pressures of contemporary life', and like Hobsbaum he feels that insufficient attention has been given to the poem's tone, which is elegiac and melancholy: 'there is a feeling that for humankind the idyllic life the horses enjoy is no longer possible'. Timms makes a very shrewd comment that Larkin has to employ the horses as an image of this idyllic life because 'we are able to imagine the ideal, but it is no longer within our expectations' (Timms, 1973, pp.74–5). He does not, however, attempt to explain our diminished expectations; to do so would be to enter into those modes of historical and sociological enquiry which are inimical to practical criticism.

Timm's book is still very helpful and informative as an introductory guide to Larkin's work and it does attempt to explain what it means by the 'perennial' themes of poetry. Hence, 'Death and age, two of Larkin's most obsessive themes, come to us whether we have grown up in post- or pre-war England' (Timms, 1973, p.89). This is, of course, true, but what Timms fails to mention is that ideas and beliefs about such things as death and age do *not* remain the same in all ages. Larkin's attitudes to death and age are not the same as those of John Keats composing his 'Ode to a Nightingale' in 1819. Larkin's response is shaped and informed by a very different set of moral and cultural values, and therefore to speak of such 'themes' as 'universal' is to ignore the particular context in which they occur. Another obvious shortcoming of thematic criticism is its tendency to ignore or play down the progression and development of ideas throughout a writer's career, usually in the interests of unity and consistency. In his discussion of 'Vers de Société', a poem written in 1971, Timms provides an appropriate example:

> The poem shows how constant Larkin's themes have remained since 1946: disappointment in life, the pressures of society on the individual, the desire to escape those pressures together with the fear of the isolation such escape brings, the encroachment of time. (Timms, 1973, p.124)

Later in this book it will be argued that 'the pressures of society on the individual' merits consideration as something more than a theme. What is important here is the way in which Larkin's poems are flattened out into a uniform body of work, with little regard for the relationship between the poems and a rapidly changing social context.

In *An Uncommon Poet for the Common Man* (1974) Lolette Kuby attempts to refashion a familiar concern with 'the human condition' by dressing it up in flimsy philosophical clothes. Accordingly, she is able to make the grand claim that 'All of Larkin's themes, sub-themes, subjects, ideas, even his style are particles of a major, unifying vision – the duality of man'. In the context of Larkin's all-embracing grasp of Western philosophy, the twentieth century is just an incidental affair. Because Larkin's 'universal themes' are 'true at any time in all places', the present functions largely as the 'atmosphere' in which 'man's essential dualism' is acted out (Kuby, 1974, pp.81, 123). The book rarely gets beyond a repetitive account of the dualistic tension between the ideal and the real, free will and fate, life and death.

Bruce Martin's book (1978) promises something more than a thesis about the human condition. It opens with a careful focus on the contemporary circumstances of Larkin's work and includes a stimulating reading of 'Church Going'. By referring to the 'post-post-Christian world' of the poem, Martin distinguishes contemporary agnosticism from earlier forms of disbelief. He notes that the speaker of the poem is 'skeptical of the fruits of skepticism' and seemingly 'as dissatisfied with his disbelief as with conventional dogma' (Martin, 1978, p.40). What is unfortunate is that, having established a precise context for his discussion of the poems, Martin should settle for a version of Kuby's 'dualism' and argue that 'Larkin's concern with a human world caught up in time, desire and

disappointment connects him with the whole line of western philosophy dealing with the distinction between the ideal and the real'
(Martin, 1978, p.49). This does little to enhance Martin's readings
of the poems and some of his interpretations are faintly ludicrous.
'At Grass' is seen from the perspective of a speaker who projects
his ideals on to the horses: 'His noticing the horses in this way
suggests regret that man cannot be like them. The poem reminds
us how hopelessly unlike the horses we are' (Martin, 1978, p.88).
Martin acknowledges the limitations of a narrowly thematic and
formalist criticism and appreciates 'the need for some kind of critical
pluralism', but his own approach falls short of this ideal (Martin,
1978, p.142).

The aim of Simon Petch in *The Art of Philip Larkin* (1981) is to
illuminate 'the subtlety and sophistication' of the poet's technique
(Petch, 1981, p.11). Once again, however, this formalist emphasis is
based upon a monotonous range of themes. *The Less Deceived* is
easily summarised:

> The unity of the poems in this book, which may seem to be belied
> by their diversity of manner, can be traced to a hard core of
> thematic concerns: the human sense of identity, the images of the
> past and the illusions of the future that we cherish and distort, our
> unawareness of the essential seriousness of so much of what we do.
> (Petch, 1981, p.60)

What is most valuable in Petch's study, and what gives it a
distinctive focus, is its concern with Larkin's use of a speaker whose
credibility varies from poem to poem. This is a useful antidote to
those biographical readings of the poems which fail to make any
distinction between poet and persona and so evaluate the work in
terms of what they imagine to be Larkin's personal lifestyle. Some of
Petch's readings are more effective than others; those poems like 'Mr
Bleaney' or 'Dockery and Son' which employ a first-person narrative
lend themselves very well to his analysis. Similarly, Petch is able to
offer good reasons why Larkin's more polemical efforts, such as
'Going, Going' and 'Homage to a Government', lack conviction.
'Church Going' is discussed in terms of a debate between two
speakers, and 'At Grass' is considered for the way in which 'an
authoritative presence' directs the reader towards a particular
interpretation.

In some ways, Petch's method resembles that of *reception theory* or *reader-response criticism*; it concentrates, for instance, on the rhetorical strategies by which certain responses are prompted from the reader. Unlike reception theory, however, it assumes that the text has a single, determinate meaning which the speaker coerces or persuades the reader into accepting. Petch does not allow for the possible divergent responses of different readers in different contexts. Sometimes his interpretations seem too restrictive. He insists, for instance, that the horses at the end of 'At Grass' are 'in no sense symbolic'; rather, they have escaped the fictions imposed on them in their racing days: 'Liberated from the past and from the demands of time, they have finally become themselves in a pastoral world of innocence and permanence' (Petch, 1981, p.59–60). This sounds rather too much like the critic imposing his own set of fictions on the poem, and the ultimate shortcoming of the book is that we learn very little about the extent to which the poems engage with the social realities of their time. Typical of Petch's generalising approach is his remark that the East Yorkshire landscape of 'Here' comes to stand for 'the random juxtaposition of beauty and beastliness which is contemporary England'. The element of myth in Petch's thinking is all too apparent.

Terry Whalen's *Philip Larkin and English Poetry* (1986) is 'primarily a practical criticism exploration of Larkin's poetry', and as such it suffers from the defects of practical criticism already outlined in this chapter. Whalen's claim that Larkin is 'a more explorative and open poet than first thoughts might suggest ... a poet whose range of vision is wider than many have perceived' is a welcome contribution to the critical debate, but the familiar emphasis on Larkin's 'sensitivity to the sadness of the human condition' does not take us very far (Whalen, 1986, pp.2, 7, 26). Judged by this standard, 'At Grass' is 'a poem about old age' and 'Bleaney represents a great deal of reality' (Whalen, 1986, pp.6, 106). Whalen goes through the routine listing of Larkin's themes, including 'failure, the fragility of human choices (between bachelorhood and marriage, for instance), the importance of vocation in life, the horrifying reality of death, the struggles of common humanity, and the universality of human misery and sadness'. It is obvious, Whalen argues, that Larkin echoes many of Samuel Johnson's concerns 'as they have a bearing on contemporary life' (Whalen, 1986, p.33). The emphasis here is very telling: these 'themes' are not regarded in any way as a *product* of contemporary life'. So intent is Whalen on demonstrating Larkin's indebtedness to 'the Augustan example' that he proceeds to talk about the plight of 'the eighteenth-century rape victim' in 'Deceptions' (Whalen, 1986, p.39). This lack of historical accuracy is one of the inevitable consequences of discussing poems predominantly in terms of literary influence. Larkin, in Whalen's estimate, is not just a 'Johnsonian analyst of the human mind'; he is also a Lawrentian romantic deeply concerned with spiritual health (Whalen, 1986, pp.40, 55). 'Wedding Wind' and 'The Explosion' are found to contain 'rare moments of experiential surprise' and a language which is both domestic and religious, but other critics are just as likely to attribute these qualities to a different set of 'modernist' influences, as we will see later ('Modernism and Symbolism', p.51) (Whalen, 1986, p.75). The problem is that literary criticism of this kind invites a mode of stylistic and thematic comparison that does not ultimately further our understanding of the very different historical contexts in which the language of poetry operates. The echoes and allusions within and between texts are endless and in themselves constitute a very limited kind of knowledge. The most impressive analysis in Whalen's book is his reading of 'Dublinesque', in which a close attention to the poem's presentation of Dublin life and culture clearly outweighs any attempt to 'place' it in terms of previous literary modes and traditions.

Thematic criticism tends to be unrewarding because it either reduces the potential meanings of a literary text to a narrow and monotonous range of 'topics', or it restricts itself to a formalist reading in which the writer's 'treatment' of a particular 'theme' is compared with that of other writers in a chosen 'tradition'. In both cases, the approach is essentially unhistorical; it assumes that a writer's 'greatness' is the product of an inherent and unswerving instinct for dealing with 'the big subjects' – birth, love, age, death – and therefore encourages the idea that these subjects are 'timeless' and 'universal'. Such themes do, of course, have an enduring relevance and appeal, but they are part of a changing *history* of ideas and beliefs and can only be fully understood in terms of that context; they do not possess the *same* meaning and significance for *every* generation of readers.

To acknowledge that 'death' is a major theme in Larkin's poetry achieves very little and hardly encourages a searching criticism of his work. As John Osborne has argued, Larkin's writing is altogether 'more contradictory, subversive and disquieting' than this old-fashioned literary criticism has supposed: 'Of course, the fact that each of us owes nature a death is not a new theme in literature. What is new – and drastic – is the extent to which it renders all else provisional.' The idea of death in Larkin's poetry is powerfully iconoclastic, toppling 'one after another of those cherished beliefs and institutions' – marriage, the family, religion – and upsetting 'every conventional piety and ideal' (Osborne, 1987, pp.184–6). What is important, as John Osborne's essay suggests, is that Larkin's ideas should not be regarded as 'universal themes', which makes for a bland and uniform criticism, but should be understood in terms of their own contemporary context, in which they are more likely to appear strange and alarming than reassuring.

Linguistic Approaches

Some of the most powerful arguments against practical criticism in the past few years have come from that branch of linguistic and literary study known as *stylistics*. For all its emphasis on a close reading of the text, practical criticism seemed to assume that the relationship between language and reality was essentially stable and unproblematic. Literary texts were therefore seen to 'reflect' the way things were, and this idea of 'mimesis' or imitation was taken for granted. Linguists, however, argued that such criticism encouraged students to produce an impressionistic response to the text, based on a generalised notion of the human condition and a simplistic model of how language communicates meaning. Ronald Carter was among those who voiced a concern about the shortcomings of practical criticism: 'Meaning is measured against an ostensibly common life experience; there is only minimal appeal to the medium from which the text is constructed' (Carter, 1982, p.3). What the study of literary texts requires, in his view, is a more principled analysis and systematic awareness of how language operates in its many different contexts. Whereas practical criticism concentrates narrowly on the text as a source of meaning, practical stylistics takes as its starting point a much broader knowledge of the rules and conventions of linguistic communication in a variety of situations, both written and spoken. One of the principal effects of stylistics is to 'demystify' the literary text: to see it essentially as 'language in use'.

An instructive example of stylistic criticism is Henry Widdowson's reading of 'Mr Bleaney'. Widdowson's basic argument is that an appreciation of how the poem functions is best served by an understanding of its grammatical features, particularly its use of person, tense and syntax. He notes that two scenes are presented in the poem: the speaker's conversation with the landlady (down to the beginning of line 10) and the speaker's private reflections on his own existence. In the first scene Mr Bleaney is regarded with detachment, but in the second scene his presence is invoked with a new sense of relationship and involvement. In the transition, there seems to be a fusion of person and tense; the first-person present of the speaker merges with the third-person past of Mr Bleaney. There is also a noticeable change in syntax, marked by the opening conjunction of the final two stanzas. What is unusual about these two stanzas is that they consist of a single complex sentence introduced by what appears to be a conditional clause. Widdowson points out that this 'If' clause is, in fact, a strange syntactic hybrid, a cross between the following two statements:

1   *If he stood here, he would see the clouds.*
2   *I do not know if he stood here and saw the clouds.*

The sequence of the final lines invites one possible meaning, while the overall structure of the two stanzas invites another. The effect of this is to disorient the reader in a way that suggests the speaker's confused thoughts and attitudes. The final three words of the poem – 'I don't know' – are 'an expression of resignation to a general state of unknowing, a failure to understand'. Widdowson shows, then, how the poem moves 'from confident detachment to confused involvement', and how this progression is conveyed through specific linguistic devices (Widdowson, 1982, p.24). He does not impose a final interpretation on the poem, nor does he seek to evaluate it in terms of artistic achievement. Instead, he suggests how the poem might be described in relation to 'normal language use', and how certain poetic effects are created by a departure from this norm.

In a similar way, David Lodge argues that what distinguishes a literary text from other forms of discourse is that it 'foregrounds' (or calls attention to) its own linguistic features. Lodge, however, places himself in a tradition of *structural linguistics* by borrowing from Roman Jakobson the idea of an opposition between two poetic styles or structures of language, namely *metaphor* and *metonomy*. Metaphor is a figure of substitution based on similarity, as when we substitute the phrase 'ships ploughed the sea' for 'ships crossed the sea'. Metonomy and the closely associated figure of *synechdoche* function by substituting an attribute or quality for the thing itself or part of the object for the whole. In the phrase 'keels crossed the deep', for instance, 'keels' is synechdoche and 'deep' is metonomy. Metonomy involves a combination of elements within the same sequence or context (ships – sea), while metaphor involves a selection of elements from a different sequence or context, as the word 'ploughed' clearly suggests (Lodge, 1977, p.74).

Lodge develops Jakobson's assertion that Romantic writing is essentially metaphoric and realist writing metonymic by extending his use of these terms into a classification of twentieth-century literature. Assuming that literary history is cyclical and repetitive, Lodge argues that 1930s writing was basically antimodernist, realistic and metonymic, while 1940s writing was modernist, symbolist and metaphoric. In the 1950s, he claims, the pendulum swung back again to produce the Movement poets who were essentially realistic and metonymic. There is no question in Lodge's mind that Larkin is antimodernist, though he concedes that Larkin *is* experimental in 'displacing lyric poetry (an inherently metaphoric mode) towards the metonymic pole' (Lodge, 1977, p.120). He proceeds to point out how Larkin employs the techniques of the realist novel, using metonymic and synechdochic detail to evoke the race-day scene in the third stanza of 'At Grass' ('Silks at the start: against the sky / Numbers and parasols . . .'). He comments on the scarcity of metaphor in Larkin's work and notes that while some of the early poems, such as 'Next, Please' or 'Toads', might be seen as extended metaphors, many poems have no metaphors at all: 'Myxomatosis', 'Poetry of Departures', 'Days', 'As Bad as a Mile', 'Afternoons'. In what Lodge considers to be Larkin's 'finest and most characteristic poems', metaphors are 'foregrounded' against a predominantly metonymic background. In 'The Whitsun Weddings', for instance, the scenery of the train journey is evoked largely by metonymy and synechdoche ('drifting breadth', 'blinding windscreens', etc.). What he finds unusual about the poem is that the final stanza suddenly 'takes off' into a more affirmative element suggested by the metaphor of the rain shower: 'This metaphor, with its mythical, magical and archaic resonances, is powerful partly because it is so different from anything else in the poem . . .' (Lodge, 1977, pp.123–5).

Larkin, then, is able to surprise us by allowing a current of metaphorical language into the poem.

Something similar happens in 'Mr Bleaney', Lodge claims, though here the effect comes not so much from the introduction of metaphor as from 'a subtle complication of metre, line-endings and syntax'. His analysis of the poem is very similar to Widdowson's: he notes that the long periodic sentence at the end of the poem marks a shift in attitude, from the persona's 'satiric spleen' to the collapse of his own morale, and he suggests that the burgeoning subordinate clauses and accumulating negatives of the final two stanzas create 'a sense of hopelessness and entrapment' (Lodge, 1977, pp.126–7). Both Widdowson and Lodge entertain the idea that language can imitate (if not simply 'reflect') a reality outside itself, and at times their critical procedures may seem very close to those of practical criticism, but both are reacting against traditional literary methods by attempting to describe linguistic effects in a more precise and analytical fashion. Lodge, for instance, sees the subject of 'death' in Larkin's poems not simply as a 'theme', but as 'a nonverbal reality'; what impresses him most is Larkin's 'paradoxical feat' in expressing that reality (Lodge, 1977, p.127). It must be pointed out that structuralist criticism does not usually accept that language functions in the 'expressive' way that Lodge suggests. Lodge's project is to revitalise rather than displace traditional literary criticism by selectively accommodating the techniques of structural linguistics. While a scrupulous preoccupation with linguistic categories might seem to give literary criticism a new claim to intellectual seriousness and rigour, the method seems curiously reticent about the social and cultural significance of 'literature'. Neither Widdowson's stylistic criticism nor Lodge's modified structuralism gets very close to issues of interpretation. Lodge's ultimate concern would seem to be with the classification or 'typology' of modern literature, and the rather laboured distinction between metaphor and metonomy seems to yield very little that is new.

A full-length structuralist approach to Larkin's poetry can be found in Guido Latré's *Locking Earth to the Sky* (1985). Following Lodge's example, Latré is principally interested in Larkin's conflicting registers of language and in the unusual conjunction of metaphoric and metonymic modes. He believes, however, that the dynamic relationship between metaphoric and metonymic principles often leads to a third, symbolic mode which reveals itself in the hidden structures of many poems:

> A typical example is the seemingly metonymical description of the horses in 'At Grass'; in this poem, the realistic description in each stanza is structured according to a pattern of standstill, incipient movement developing to a climax, subsequent rest and final standstill. When taken on its own, this motif is metaphoric; it functions as a vehicle of time's progress in human life. Simultaneously, however, such patterns are based on metonymical contiguities which do not seem to result from the poet's artistic transformation; like 'At Grass', most of the symbolic poems remain realistic. (Latré, 1985, p.437)

The casual reference to 'time's progress in human life' suggests that this kind of criticism shows as little interest in historical context as some of the more traditional approaches already discussed. Latré goes much further than Lodge in classifying the predominant types of metaphor and metonomy in Larkin's work, but many readers are likely to be unimpressed by the discovery of 'contiguous horizontal isotopies' in 'Ambulances' or 'spatial contiguity' and 'particularizing Pi-synechdoche' in 'Here' (Latré, 1985, pp.168, 182). Even so, Latré brings some interesting new insights to the study of Larkin's poetry, and his reading of 'Here' demonstrates very well how the metonymic mode becomes symbolic.

In 'Here', Latré argues, there is a patterning which is convincingly based on realistic or metonymic detail, but which nevertheless manages to lift the poem's meaning beyond that of realistic catalogue. He identifies three symmetrical phases, each of which is based on the movement from town to country. In each case, there is 'an identical patterning of the sentences around the skeleton of three propositions: FROM – THROUGH – TO', hence the residents in stanza two come *from* 'raw estates' and 'Push *through* plateglass swing doors *to* their desires' (italics added). Along with this prepositional pattern, Latré observes 'a corresponding substantial structure of places of departure, passage and destination'. Each place of destination holds an abstract promise but is successively 'reduced' to the sum of its material parts and becomes, in its turn, a new place of departure. The traveller's journey seems to have a cyclical pattern which lacks any final destination: 'the traveller has to go on swerving because each destiny is never a final destiny'. Latré does not attempt to explain the impulse behind the poem's journey, but he succeeds in showing how 'the changing point of reference leaves the observer indefinite and literally unsettled', and he also reveals how images of light and water create an impression of both linear and cyclical patterning (Latré, 1985, pp.223–7). In his reference to 'cyclical wanderings' in 'Here', Latré hints at the poem's possible relationships with classical myths and archetypes, and also shows how literary theory might draw on the structuralist anthropology of such thinkers as Claude Lévi-Strauss, as well as on the more familiar structuralist linguistics of Roman Jakobson and others.

Latré's conclusion is that Larkin's poems are 'very often in search of the symbolic moment in which mimesis of reality (metonomy) and creative transformation (metaphor) intersect' (Latré, 1985, p.438). He admits that part of his intention is to reformulate the main trends in traditional Larkin scholarship in structuralist terms, and to some extent his recognition of a symbolic mode of writing draws on recent claims that Larkin is working partly within a tradition of symbolist poetry going back to the work of W.B. Yeats and nineteenth-century French writers (see 'Modernism and Symbolism', p.51). Latré, however, sees symbolism not as a matter of 'influence' but as an element of grammatical structure.

Ultimately, then, it would seem that the stylistic and structuralist approaches reviewed in this chapter are as narrowly formalist as the most ardent practical criticism. While being intensely preoccupied with features of grammar and syntax, these approaches show very little regard for the social and historical contexts in which poetry is written and read. It would be wrong, however, to think that all linguistic criticism operated in this way. Roger Fowler is as concerned as other linguists about the deficiencies of conventional literary criticism, but wishes to go much further than just describing the formal structures which give texts their shape and function. 'It is a mistake', he argues, 'to regard literary texts as autonomous patterns of linguistic form cut off from social forces' (Fowler, 1981, p.7). He challenges the idea (espoused by Widdowson and by Lodge) that there is a distinct difference between poetic or 'literary' language and 'ordinary' language. Literature, he insists, is a form of *discourse*, a language activity within a particular social structure and therefore as amenable to linguistic study as other forms of discourse such as letters and advertisements.

Fowler's main argument is that literary texts, like other varieties of linguistic usage, have both social determinants and social consequences: they are shaped by prevailing social and cultural values but also read and understood within particular social and institutional contexts. There is, accordingly, a powerful interrelationship between linguistic structures and social structures. In Fowler's linguistic criticism, the structural form of a poem constitutes a *representation* of the world; the text does not simply 'reflect' reality but rather contains specific versions or possible interpretations of reality. Put more simply, 'style' embodies a view of the world. Literature, like other forms of discourse, is scored through with competing and conflicting ideas and values. The critic's task is to understand linguistically how these versions of 'the real' are constructed and what their consequences might be. Fowler's approach is based largely on a *sociolinguistic* theory which views the different varieties or registers within one language as enshrining variant world views. The values and beliefs of a particular social class, for instance, tend to be coded in its linguistic structures. Because Fowler's method sees language in relation to social contexts and their historical development, it might also be described as a *materialist* theory. The idea of literature as *social discourse* can offer us valuable insights into Larkin's poetry. Fowler has not written specifically on the work of Philip Larkin, but his linguistic criticism will be adopted in the Appraisal section of this book (Part Two). At this stage it is worth illustrating how *discourse theory* might be applied to individual poems.

A good start in this direction was made some years ago by Jonathan Raban in *The Society of the Poem* (1971). Although Raban refers to language as 'the medium' of literature (to Fowler, literature *is* language), he nevertheless claims that 'the language of the poem is the language of society at large' (Raban, 1971, p.27). He proceeds to 'map out the social geography' of poetry, asking if poetic order corresponds in any way to social order. In his first example, 'Mr Bleaney', he notices 'some sort of tussle going on between the social dimension of the verse and the verbal patterns into which it is arranged' (Raban, 1971, pp.29–30). He draws our attention to the staple iambic pentameter and the recurring monosyllabic rhymes, but then notes that the speech patterns seem to jar against this traditional form. The opening two words of the poem, for instance, make up a trochaic rather than iambic foot, and a similar reversal of stress occurs in the last line of the first stanza with 'Fall to'. The voice of the landlady cuts against the metrical pattern of the verse with a rush of unaccented syllables: 'The whole time he was at the Bodies'. Raban interprets this clash of speech patterns and verse patterns in terms of social class, pointing to the condescending irony with which the narrator responds to the seemingly predictable clichés of the landlady and also remarking upon the slang which Mr Bleaney is imagined to have used: 'stub my fags' and 'why / He kept on plugging at the four aways'. Like other commentators, however, Raban perceives a shift in rhetorical intensity at the beginning of stanza six. Here, the iambic beat seems to slow down and become more regular, the vocabulary becomes more figurative, the line endings start to coincide with syntactical pauses, and the tone becomes more assured and more resonant. Raban interprets this shift in register as the 'hallowed and formal language of poetry' recovering momentum and seeking to impose order over the other disparate voices in the earlier stanzas. What finally hinders this process is the shrug of the final three words, 'I don't know', which is 'anticipated, built in, even at the poem's highest point of rhetorical richness and assurance'.

Raban does not see the conflation of voices and registers in the poem as a weakness; rather he sees 'Mr Bleaney' as 'a remarkably successful example of a poem which is very much like a political democracy of a peculiarly muddled and English kind' (Raban, 1971, p.32). Raban is mistaken in identifying the final two stanzas as 'the essentially aristocratic voice of "poetry"', since these lines are still part of the narrator's speech. What he means, presumably, is that the closing lines are closer to traditional English lyricism than the earlier dialogue between landlady and lodger. In this respect, his suggestion that the poem strives for order and authority over the individual lives and voices it represents is a very revealing one. Raban is equating what he sees as a compromised settlement with a particular attitude to class relationships in modern society. The strength of his approach is not just in its careful attention to the poem as a kind of speech act but in its simultaneous awareness that linguistic structures are closely related to political and economic structures: 'I think if one were looking for a working definition of the tone of English liberalism one couldn't find a better example than "Mr Bleaney"' (Raban, 1971, p.33). This is a suggestion to which we will return in the Appraisal section (Part Two).

Modernism and Symbolism

From the outset of his career as a poet, Larkin made no secret of his hostility to the ideas and techniques of modernism. His most notorious attack on modernist art occurs in the introduction to his collection of jazz criticism, *All What Jazz*, where modernism is equated with mystification and outrage. It is here, too, that Larkin expresses his deep distaste for the work of that modernist trio, Parker, Pound and Picasso. Modernist experiments, whether in music, poetry or painting, are regarded by Larkin as 'irresponsible exploitations of technique in contradiction of human life as we know it' (Larkin, 1983, p.297). It may seem surprising, then, that the most striking development in Larkin criticism has been the insistence in the 1980s that the poetry has a profoundly 'symbolist' and, by implication, 'modernist' dimension. Whereas Donald Davie and others had sought to defend Larkin's poetry from charges of gentility and parochialism by seeking to explain and justify its seemingly limited horizons, the new Larkin criticism argues more positively that the poetry often reveals a strongly 'affirmative' and 'transcendent' element. This strain of criticism is not entirely new. Alan Brownjohn, for instance, had identified 'certain indefinable images of purity and serenity' which enabled the poet to 'rise above the soiled terrain of living' (Brownjohn, 1975, p.3). The emphasis after 1975, though, was very much on Larkin's persistent and generally unrecognised connections with European modernism, with W.B. Yeats, T.S. Eliot and the French symbolist poets.

What precipitated this new critical approach was undoubtedly the publication in 1974 of *High Windows*, a volume widely noted for its unusual experiments with form and its often unnerving obscurity and allusiveness. Clive James, reviewing the volume in *Encounter*, acknowledged Larkin as 'the poet of the void' and pointed to a significant connection between his allegedly 'circumscribed' outlook and the poetic intensity of his writing: 'The total impression of *High Windows* is of despair made beautiful. Real despair and real beauty, with not a trace of posturing in either' (James, 1979, pp.61, 51). James's response is one of shock and surprise, and his bafflement in confronting such poems as 'Livings' and 'High Windows' leads him to admit that 'Larkin can on occasion be a difficult poet' (James, 1974, p.55).

Looking back on *High Windows* in 1980, Grevel Lindop tried to assess the impact of the volume and its relationship with the earlier poems. It seemed that *High Windows* contained fewer of those 'depressive' poems where experience was tested and found wanting; instead, the tendency was to reaffirm the value of human endeavour ('To the Sea', 'Show Saturday', 'The Explosion') or to expose it to comic satire ('Posterity', 'Homage to a Government', 'This Be The Verse'). What was most startling, however, was the re-emergence of the symbolist vision which Larkin was thought to have renounced (along with the potent influence of W. B. Yeats) after the publication of *The North Ship* in 1945:

> But the striking development is the turn to symbolism rather than discursive statement. The earlier poems tend to offer stated judgements: 'how we live measures our own nature'; 'Never such innocence again'; 'Life is first boredom, then fear'. But poem after poem in *High Windows* refuses to give us anything so consolingly tangible ... Always Larkin seems to be aiming for the symbol which will resonate in the mind, calling forth harmonies that have nothing to do with the carefully limited, scrupulously precise resolutions of most of the earlier poems. (Lindop, 1980, p.50)

Lindop is referring here to poems like 'Money', 'Livings' and 'The Card-Players' – poems which are tenuous and oblique in their range of references – but also to the curious pairing of 'Sad Steps' and 'Solar', in which images of the moon and the sun are brought into close correspondence. Lindop's intention is not to elevate the 'symbolist' poems above the other works written by Larkin in the 1970s, and he reserves his highest praise for a small group of poems which eschew both symbolist experiment and satirical criticism: 'The Building', 'The Old Fools', and 'Aubade' (published separately in the *Times Literary Supplement* in December 1977).

The most impressive appraisal of Larkin's symbolist potential is undoubtedly Seamus Heaney's fine essay, 'The Main of Light', first published in *Larkin at Sixty* (Thwaite, 1982) and reprinted in *The Government of the Tongue* (1988). Heaney acknowledges Larkin's detailed social observation, but calls our attention to a simultaneous yearning for transcendence and revelation:

> Yet while Larkin is exemplary in the way he sifts the conditions of contemporary life, refuses alibis and pushes consciousness to-

wards an exposed condition that is neither cynicism nor despair, there survives in him a repining for a more crystalline reality to which he might give allegiance. When that repining finds expression something opens and moments occur which deserve to be called visionary. (Heaney, 1982, p.132)

Heaney twice uses the word 'symbolist' to describe the linguistic structures of poems in *High Windows*. He notes the unusual diction of 'Sad Steps' ('O wolves of memory, immensements!') and praises 'Solar' as a hymn to the sun in which the poet is clearly 'far from the hatless one who took off his cycle clips in awkward reverence'. It is not just in *High Windows* that Heaney observes the visionary quality of Larkin's poems. The same flooding of light occurs in earlier poems such as 'Deceptions' and 'Water'. While this luminous quality might be described as 'romantic' in its imaginative intensity, its most comparable achievements are to be found in the Anglo-Irish modernism of James Joyce and W.B. Yeats. The remote and enigmatic ending of 'Here' reminds Heaney of Joyce's conclusion to 'The Dead': 'It is an epiphany, an escape from the "scrupulous meanness" of the disillusioned intelligence'. Heaney nevertheless insists upon the peculiar Englishness of Larkin's poetry: 'At Grass', 'MCMXIV', 'How Distant' and 'The Explosion' are born of an 'elysian' mood and might be regarded as modern visions of 'the old Platonic England', a poetic dream world that has its roots in medieval romance (Heaney, 1982, p.137).

Whereas Heaney places Larkin's poems within a literary continuum that gives them claims to both twentieth-century modernism and a much older poetic tradition, Barbara Everett insists upon their post-modern or post-symbolist qualities. In 'Philip Larkin: After Symbolism' (1980) she argues that Larkin's poetry declares its difference not by evading or ignoring modernism but by actively engaging with it. For all Larkin's disclaimers about modernism, his work shows unusual affinities with that of T.S. Eliot and the French symbolist poets. The most persuasive aspect of Everett's article is her reading of Larkin's 'Sympathy in White Major', a poem which parodies Théophile Gautier's 'Symphonie en blanc majeure' while employing the same techniques. Everett argues effectively that the poem cannot be fully appreciated without some knowledge of a French symbolist tradition that encompasses the poetry of Charles Baudelaire and Stéphane Mallarmé, as well as the series of paintings by James McNeill Whistler titled 'Symphony in White'. The purpose of these echoes, she claims, is to deliver a warning about the moral dangers of 'art for art's sake'. The speaker of the poem is a solipsistic figure who appears to deliver a toast to himself and his own achievements. As George Hartley has pointed out, the closing lines of the poem – '*Here's to the whitest man I know* – / Though white is not my favourite colour' – turn on the ambiguity of 'whiteness'. 'The whitest man' is a phrase from the days of the British Raj (one of obvious approval) and one that was flaunted in the Edwardian music hall. Whiteness, however, also implies a lack of experience and a degree of moral cowardice. Hartley refers to 'the white feather sent to the Major who wouldn't volunteer for active service' (Hartley, 1988, pp.305–6). In keeping with other poems in *High Windows*, 'Sympathy in White Major' is a mocking, sardonic account of the tension between self-interest and social commitment. Everett admits that the poem is intensely English in its clichés but maintains that it is predominantly an ironic and playful conversion of a characteristically symbolist idiom.

'High Windows', too, is thought by Barbara Everett to employ some of the ideas and techniques of French symbolist poetry. The closing lines depicting 'the deep blue air' are reminiscent of Mallarmé's 'most consistent and philosophical symbol' – 'L'azur' ('the blue') – which embodies both the necessity and the absence of the ideal. Larkin's poem, like Mallarmé's 'Les Fenêtres' ('The Windows'), sees the sky as imprinted with human longing for fulfilment (Everett, 1980, p.237). Everett is not implying that Larkin merely imitates French symbolist writers, but rather that he employs a range of symbols only to record their current unavailability or to counter the idealism that they formerly represented. In one sense, then, he might well be regarded as an anti-symbolist poet making ironic use of symbolist ideas and techniques. Nevertheless, an important aspect of Everett's argument is that a good deal of Larkin's work – as far back as *The Less Deceived* – suggests a knowledgeable interest in French poetry. 'Arrivals, Departures' might well be an imitation of Baudelaire's 'Le Port', while 'Toads' brings to mind the Chimaeras of Baudelaire's 'Chacun sa Chimère'.

Andrew Motion's *Philip Larkin* (1982) was the first full-length study of Larkin's work to explore its symbolist dimensions. Motion agrees with Everett that Larkin had certainly responded to the example of French symbolist poets at an early stage. We are reminded that one of Larkin's earliest poems, 'Femmes Damnées', takes its title from Baudelaire, and that Larkin commented on the closing line of 'Absences' ('Such attics cleared of me! Such absences!') that it sounded like 'a slightly-unconvincing translation from a French symbolist' (Motion, 1982, p.74). The main argument in Motion's book, however, is concerned with the persistent and combined influence of Thomas Hardy and W.B. Yeats. In the 1966 reissue of *The North Ship* Larkin claims that an early infatuation with Yeats gave way after 1945 to the example of Thomas Hardy. The poem 'Waiting for breakfast', he suggests, 'shows the Celtic fever abated and the patient sleeping soundly' (Larkin, 1983, p.30). Contending with this version of events, Motion suggests that the symbolist element in Yeats was absorbed much more thoroughly than Larkin himself admits, and that it often provides a powerful emotional charge. Larkin's 'best' and most characteristic work might be regarded as a dialectic between the empirical mode of Hardy and the symbolist mode of Yeats, the language of sadness and isolation repeatedly vying with the language of aspiration and transcendence. In Motion's view, this dialectic is an expression of the poet's divided response to the world; it shapes and informs 'a continual debate between hopeful romantic yearning and disillusioned pragmatism' (Motion, 1982, p.38).

In his readings of the poems, Motion ranges extensively from *The North Ship* to *High Windows*, drawing our attention to those moments when rational argument and logical progression break down and give way to a bizarre and seemingly unrelated discourse. The image of 'sand-clouds' at the end of 'Dockery and Son' is a brief but telling example. The same structural features are evident in 'Next, Please', where a dread of death is compounded with a sense of wonder. 'Dry-Point' is regarded as Larkin's 'most purely symbolist' poem, which explains why it is more susceptible to vagueness and obscurity than is usual in Larkin's work (Motion, 1982, p.76).

Like Barbara Everett, Motion believes that *The Whitsun Weddings* is 'the book that conforms most exactly to the attitudes and styles associated with the Movement' and therefore the least symbolist in technique (Motion, 1982, p.77). Even so, he finds evidence of the symbolist method in the closing lines of 'Water' and 'The Whitsun Weddings'. It is worth noting here that the frequent equation between 'symbolism' and 'transcendence' perhaps leads Motion to stress the 'positive' or 'affirmative' aspects of 'The Whitsun

Weddings' rather more than other critics have done: 'Larkin overcomes his sense of himself as an outsider. He is released from the empirically observed world, and its attendant disappointments, into one of transcendent imaginative fulfilment' (Motion, 1982, p.78). Motion goes on to argue that *High Windows* contains 'more purely symbolist moments' than *The Whitsun Weddings* ('Solar' and 'Money' are cited) but that this is offset by the vigorous colloquial diction and insistent factuality of the book. The poem which 'most successfully employs symbolist techniques' is 'High Windows', which illustrates very well the accelerated shifts between different registers of language and different modes of perception (Motion, 1982, pp.79, 81).

Motion's book was undoubtedly a welcome contribution to Larkin criticism and effectively challenged the common assumption that what Larkin wrote was a poetry severely limited in outlook and unadventurous in style and technique. Yet the main argument of the book raises a number of difficulties, as does the whole conception of a symbolist dimension in Larkin's poetry. To begin with, it would seem that the relationship between Hardy and Yeats as opposing influences – one empirical and the other symbolist – is too neatly polarised. As Tom Paulin has argued in *Thomas Hardy: The Poetry of Perception*, it is unwise to equate Hardy's poems with a strictly empirical outlook, since there are those occasions when the language might well be described as 'visionary'. In other words, Hardy's poems are not without their own affirmative and transcendent possibilities. Paulin demonstrates very well how the 'visionary images' in such poems as 'The Whitsun Weddings', 'Money' and 'High Windows' might just as well be attributed to the example of Hardy as that of Yeats (Paulin, 1986, p.32). On the other hand, to refer to Yeats repeatedly in terms of hopeful aspiration and imaginative transcendence can be equally misleading and simplifying. Yeats undoubtedly has his share of disillusionment, isolation and sadness.

Central to Motion's thesis is the assertion that Hardy and Yeats are broadly representative of a struggle that has dominated English poetry since the turn of the century: a struggle between a native English tradition, including Edward Thomas, A.E. Housman and the Georgian poets, and a more cosmopolitan, modernist tradition typified by T.S. Eliot and Ezra Pound. Motion is able to enhance and elevate Larkin's achievements by giving him the credit for having produced a synthesis of these two disparate elements in twentieth-century poetry. It is possible that Larkin himself believed in something called 'the English line' and his 1973 edition of *The Oxford Book of Twentieth-Century English Verse* would seem to confirm the idea. The problem is that literary traditions of this kind are frequently created and rarely challenged; they come to be accepted as natural and given entities rather than artificial and constructed categories. Too often aesthetic preferences disguise a particular set of cultural and political assumptions.

In the case of 'the English line', associations of a patriotic, conservative kind are readily apparent; the term implies a continuity of thought and emotion – often identified as 'the true voice of feeling' – extending through the nineteenth century from Wordsworth onwards and interrupted only by the Great War of 1914–18. Christopher Ricks and Edna Longley are among those who claim that Larkin played an important role in nourishing and sustaining this 'tradition' (Ricks, 1974, p.6; Longley, 1974, p.64). It is, of course, convenient to conceive of literary history in terms of its own inherent tensions and resolutions, but to do so is to abstract such patterns from the more complex social history in which poetry, like other forms of written and spoken discourse, is deeply implicated. In the course of actual events, there is no 'true voice of feeling', only many different and often conflicting voices.

The chief weakness of the 'symbolist' theory is that it is ultimately no more historical in its assumptions than the narrowly thematic forms of criticism discussed in 'Thematic Approaches' (p.33). Literary ideas such as 'symbolism' and 'modernism' tend to be considered as if they were free-floating concepts and not the products of a particular society at a particular time. Accordingly, the development of the poetry and the criteria by which it might be judged are regarded almost entirely in terms of competing literary movements and influences, and not in relation to a specific context. To be fair, there is a suggestion in Andrew Motion's book that the literary ambitions of Larkin and his contemporaries were 'crucially shaped by threats from abroad and deprivations and disillusionment at home' (Motion, 1982, p.29), but this pertains only to the Movement phase of Larkin's work and to the obvious manifestations of war; there is no sustained analysis of the poetry in relation to that context. Throughout the book, Larkin's use of symbolism is equated with 'freedom' and 'liberation', as if these words can be used unproblematically in the context of post-1945 England. Symbolism, we are told, offers Larkin a release from 'the empirically observed world, and its attendant disappointments', a redemption from 'distressing daily circumstances', but because symbolism is construed in very general and unhistorical terms we are never offered an explanation of why the poems yearn for transcendence or why, indeed, the empirical world should be a place of disappointment and distress (Motion, 1982, pp.78, 80).

This tendency towards an unhistorical and anti-sociological bias in Larkin criticism is apparent in Barbara Everett's most recent work. Developing Seamus Heaney's notion of an 'elysian' mood in Larkin's poetry, Everett contemplates those poetic moments that might be described as 'Edenic', when a strongly literal realism seems to give way to an intense idealism. Thus, 'The Building' is a 'public, representative statement', but it also opens up 'corridors of imagination' which link it with the work of Kafka, Dante and Virgil. The result of this enlarged framework of reference is that 'the final "All know they are going to die" leaves room within a modern monosyllabic trenchancy for a classic and monumental timelessness of statement' (Everett, 1986, p.246). Here, the terms of the earlier symbolist argument are subtly shifted and 'literariness' becomes, in itself, a guarantee of transcendental value; it is the poem's relationship with an established and respected literary tradition that elevates it beyond a merely 'social' significance. The problem is that 'The Building', like the earlier 'Church Going', is very much the product of a modern, secular consciousness and its sentiments cannot be regarded as 'timeless' without blatantly ignoring the poem's very specific cultural context. Furthermore, to insist upon the poem's 'timeless' statement is to overlook the possibility that different readers at different times will respond to its implications in diverse and changing ways.

If 'The Building' constitutes a potent image of the underworld, 'At Grass' represents for Everett 'a highly sophisticated image of Edenic innocence'. Unlike Seamus Heaney in his essay 'Englands of the Mind', Everett does not equate this elysian mood with the poem's nostalgia for a particular version of national history (Heaney, 1980, p.166). It is not the realistic, metonymic details outlined by David Lodge that attract her attention, but rather the seeming 'timelessness' of the poem: 'The horses are perceived – "The eye can hardly pick them out" – at the distant heart of that long quiet afternoon which lies both before and after the dream of human history'. At the same time, however, she wishes to see in the poem 'a figure for human innocence within the terms a civilised existence offers' (Everett, 1986, p.250). What those terms are and how they might be achieved without recourse to human history are questions that are left unanswered. These are the difficulties and contradictions of a criticism that seeks to *evade* history and which tries to isolate some pure and uncontaminated aesthetic experience from what is merely 'social'.

The critical approaches examined in this chapter have a tendency to abstract literary influences from the broader context in which poetry happens, and to assess individual poems in terms of how they relate to preconceived literary traditions. At its worst, this kind of criticism becomes a matter of highlighting obscure allusions, as if these were an assurance of the poet's intellectual command and an undoubted sign of his progressive and modernist leanings. George Hartley, the publisher of *The Less Deceived*, is among those who are persuaded by the argument, and his essay 'Not Like Us' deals with the symbolist method of such poems as 'Livings' and 'If, My Darling' (Hartley, 1988). In the same collection of essays, Edna Longley's 'Poète Maudit Manqué' looks at Larkin's posture as the accursed and outcast poet and comments on the related themes of death, corruption, fantasy and violence. 'Deceptions' and 'The Explosion' are thought to be 'Baudelairean' poems. Longley herself offers an appropriate criticism when she concedes that 'All this may seem much too torrid, erotic and exotic . . .' (Longley, 1988, p.221). The task of the Appraisal (Part Two) in this book is to suggest how and where a more responsive and responsible *historicist criticism* might begin.

Part Two:
Appraisal

Historicist Criticism

Most critical studies of Philip Larkin's poetry have tended to regard 'history' and 'society' as background information, so that the context of the writing is treated as a matter of secondary interest and importance. Alternatively, Larkin has been studied as a poet of 'social observation', as if the work simply 'reflected' society in some direct and unproblematic way. More recently, Larkin has been seen as a poet whose work 'transcends' society and acquires an affirmative value in its ability to move beyond 'mere' sociological observation. This appraisal adopts a very different approach; it presupposes that Larkin's work is deeply and perpetually implicated in history, both partaking of the values and meanings inherent in modern society, but in turn helping to shape the beliefs and ideals of its readers. Society, in this instance, is not regarded as a static entity or backdrop, but as a dynamic and changing formation, a set of institutions, practices and experiences, of which poetry, like all literature, is an essential and valuable part. Historicist criticism begins with the fundamental assumption that writing and reading take place in history, and that the meanings of any text are therefore historically variable. This is not to say that literary works have an infinite range of meanings, all of them equally valid, but rather that the scope or horizon of possible meanings is determined by the conjuncture of two historical moments: the moment of writing and the moment of reading.

The publication of Philip Larkin's *Collected Poems* allows us to see the full extent of the relationship between his writing and the changing social texture from 1938 to 1983. More than ever, there is a need for a thorough *contextual* study of Larkin's work and a detailed understanding of the complex relations between the structure of the poetry and the structure of the society in which it was written. No systematic reading of Larkin's wartime writing has been offered by critics of his work, even though it is now clear that the events of 1939–45 were crucial in determining not only the kind of poetry Larkin wished to compose but the values and ideals which it came to espouse. It is clear, too, that there are significant shaping connections between Larkin's individual books of poetry and the prevailing social attitudes of the post-war years. Anthony Hartley, in *A State of England*, claims that the two great reform movements in the post-war years were 'the establishment of the Welfare State society at home and the liquidation of the British colonial empire abroad' (Hartley, 1963, p. 12). Later historians such as Kenneth Morgan have argued that the effects of post-war reform have perhaps been overstated (Morgan, 1990), but it is nevertheless the case that the psychological and material consequences of social change after the Second World War decisively affected artistic and cultural ideals. Hartley believes that 'the main fact governing English life since 1939 – a fact so obvious that it is frequently overlooked altogether – is a loss of power' (Hartley, 1963, p. 58). It will be argued in this appraisal that 'loss of power', whether real or imagined, has a pervasive and influential role in Larkin's work.

In one sense, the relationship between Larkin's poems and their changing social context is very obvious. The language and imagery of the poems seem to operate within a public domain that we would not expect to find, for instance, in the poetry of Dylan Thomas. The strong visual imagery in Larkin's work is recognisably that of post-war England, a landscape both rural and urban, of meadows and wheatfields, cooling towers, canals, new housing estates and advertisement hoardings. The language is distinctively colloquial, employing many of the features of contemporary speech. The poems are concerned with both the changing social fabric and the changing attitudes and beliefs of post-war England, and to some extent they provide a written record of successive phases of later twentieth-century social history, from the insecurities of wartime society, through the austerity of the immediate post-war years and the new-found affluence of the late 1950s and 1960s, to the eventual fracture and anticipated break-up of the Welfare State in the remaining decades. The poems, though, are essentially 'versions' of that history and through their formal and stylistic devices they can strive to validate a particular image or idea of society or, conversely, seek to deny a certain perspective or way of looking at events.

This appraisal does not naïvely suppose that literary works can somehow grant us immediate access to history and enable us to know that history in all its complexity. What it does argue, however, is that literary texts have an important *interpretative* function. As Alan Sinfield puts it, texts are 'constructions of conceivable lives . . . interpretations and evaluations of perceived possibilities in the real world' (Sinfield, 1983, p.1). In this sense texts might be said to *intervene* in a history of ideas and meanings, and this is part of their enduring cultural value. Obviously, no literary work can ever fully *represent* the history or society it purports to deal with, however plausible and persuasive its images and interpretations of that history or society might be. It is perhaps better, then, to think of language as having a *constitutive* rather than a *representative* function. Historicist criticism tends to regard 'literature' as *social discourse*, a language activity within a particular social structure. The varieties of language found in different literary texts 'constitute' different world views or interpretations of 'reality'. In Larkin's poetry, the renovation and revigoration of traditional forms and techniques is in keeping with the ideals of the new social democracy after 1945. Despite its occasional obscurities, Larkin's poetry is generally considered to be 'accessible' and 'readerly'. One of the most interesting aspects of Larkin's work is the degree to which it readjusts the diction of English poetry by considerably extending its sociolinguistic range, including those items of vocabulary that would otherwise be regarded as slang: 'sod all', 'a load of crap', 'fucked up'. This vernacular idiom is a persistent and essential part of the texture of Larkin's writing, much more so than the occasional comic digressions – such as the Cockney pub scene – in T.S. Eliot's *The Waste Land*. Historicist criticism is frequently caricatured as crude sociological analysis, but it is usually much more sensitive to language than those forms of criticism which neglect the historical context and social function of literature.

Historicist criticism believes that the meanings of literary works are produced within the context of writing but also conditioned and modified within the context of reading. There are, however, those occasions when the events and experiences which inform poetry appear to take place in the distant past and not the present moment of composition. Among Larkin's overtly historical poems are

'MCMXIV', 'How Distant', 'The Card-Players' and 'Livings'. Perhaps the best example is 'Deceptions', a poem that announces its historiographical nature with a quotation from Henry Mayhew's *London Labour and the London Poor* (1861), based on an interview with a London prostitute. As Graham Holderness has demonstrated, the poem's 'reference back' to a historical era other than its own creates innumerable difficulties of interpretation and therefore constitutes a significant challenge to *any* critical approach. In a very effective pedagogic exercise, Holderness stages an imaginary discussion of 'Deceptions' among four literary critics of different theoretical persuasions. Predictably, Cleanth (a formalist in the practical/ new criticism mode) insists that 'the poem should not *mean* but *be*', and wishes to see it as 'a vivid realisation of experience in poetic language', regardless of its nineteenth-century setting. Cleanth does, however, have some perceptive remarks to make about the imagery of 'Deceptions':

> The images of wounding, of light, and the concrete precision of 'your mind lay open like a drawer of knives' all work together to convey the sensations of something vulnerable that has been forced open, dragged out into the hard light, left exposed as a self-tormenting consciousness filled with sharp humiliation, unable to close. (Holderness, 1989, p.124)

Raymond, a Marxist, concentrates on what the poem reveals about the history of Victorian England: 'a world of extreme contrasts between wealth and poverty; a world of deprivation and undeserved suffering; a world of cruelty and exploitation' (Holderness, 1989, p.125). Kate, a feminist critic, shows what is lacking in Raymond's narrow historical reading by insisting that the poem's preoccupation with Victorian England should not distract us from its actual modern context (the context in which it was written) or prevent us from reading it through our own contemporary perspectives: 'The essential point is that Larkin in 1950 was apparently able to consider rape as a matter of "desire": and to use that assumption as the basis for a sympathetic representation of the rapist' (Holderness, 1989, p.127). Colin, a poststructuralist, denies that the poem is a 'representation' of 'real experience', since 'the effort to capture a reality beyond language is doomed to failure'. The title 'Deceptions' is 'an ironic reflection on the poem itself' and its own self-reflexive fictional status. The text never pretends to be anything other than a poem in 1950, 'using a Victorian sociological document to tell a story about Victorian life' (Holderness, 1989, p.128). Holderness demonstrates very well the *plurality* of literary criticism but shows just as effectively the difficulties involved in any attempt to reconcile the variety of possible theoretical approaches. 'Deceptions' is a provocative and disturbing poem, and the diverse readings it has prompted support the idea that criticism is a debate in which meanings and interpretations are continually challenged and contested.

A much more extensive and informed historicist critique of 'Deceptions' than the brief and necessarily tentative reading attributed to 'Raymond' has been proposed by John Goode. The strength of John Goode's reading is that it is able to accommodate a range of critical perspectives within a predominantly historicist approach. His essay is sensitive to images of light in 'Deceptions', linking these to ideas of distance and also to the problems of realising and representing past experiences in language, but it also suggests how the speaker's recognition of his own 'limitations' determines the sexual politics of the poem: 'he is deceived because he feels, most strongly, not the suffering, but the disgusting violence of male desire'. In this reading, the irony of the poem is 'intensely, even bitterly, self-critical'. Goode shows how an informed knowledge of the poem's source in Mayhew can illuminate its levels of meaning, and he argues persuasively that the speaker's limited viewpoint is implicitly linked, via that of Mayhew, 'with the moral limitations of bourgeois society which believes itself to be philanthropic' (Goode, 1988, p.134). At the same time, we need to understand the poem in terms of its own historical context. As 'Fables of Freedom' (see p.80) suggests, the poem's 'way of seeing' is informed by the passive and quietistic attitudes which characterised a good deal of post-war culture and which generally determined the outlook of *The Less Deceived*.

It should be clear, then, that historicist criticism does not apply only to those works that explore an overtly 'historical' subject matter. Nor is historicist criticism narrowly preoccupied with the extent to which literary texts confirm or disconfirm some preconceived and unalterable idea of history. As Hans Robert Jauss has argued, both writing *and* reading take place in history: 'A literary work is not an object that stands by itself and that offers the same view to each reader in each period. It is not a monument that monologically reveals its timeless essence' (Jauss, 1982, p.21).

Clearly, this kind of historical enquiry challenges the traditional assumption that great works of literature contain a timeless, universal wisdom about the human condition or a single, determinate meaning that holds good for all readers. What historicist criticism proposes instead is a notion of cultural value based on the pleasures and insights that derive from an encounter with language in its changing contexts of writing and reading. An informed historical reading of the poetry seeks to understand the relationship between the structures of language and the prevailing structures of belief and meaning; it seeks a knowledge of how rhetorical and stylistic devices continue to provoke the responses of a diverse and changing readership. In this respect, to read the poetry historically is to enquire about its value and meaning at the present time, and to read it in terms of how it might challenge and transform, rather than merely confirm, our settled opinions about the world.

Larkin's Wartime Writings

It is commonly assumed that Larkin's first 'major' collection of poems was *The Less Deceived* (1955). For this reason, very little serious attention has been given to the earlier writings of the 1940s. Most commentators have referred to *The North Ship* (1945) as an immature and derivative work, marred by introspection, obscurity and overwrought romanticism. Larkin's introduction to the 1966 reissue of *The North Ship* has encouraged the idea that the substitution of Thomas Hardy for W.B. Yeats as a dominant influence was directly responsible for a more colloquial, ironic and empirical style of writing. The counter argument, as we have seen, is that the influence of W.B. Yeats, far from being defunct, continued to shape a poetry of symbolist intensity and transcendental yearning. What both patterns of development overlook, however, is that by 1945 Larkin had produced a substantial body of work, only part of which eventually saw publication in *The North Ship*. What the unpublished poems reveal, importantly, is that the formative influences on Larkin's work had less to do with the presence of Yeats and Hardy than with the prevailing attitudes and techniques of such poets as W.H. Auden and Louis MacNeice. Most significantly, it is in Larkin's wartime writings that the impact of 'the Auden generation' is clearly evident.

The publication of Larkin's *Collected Poems* has revealed that the esoteric, introspective nature of *The North Ship* was not simply a product of poetic immaturity but largely a consequence of the social and political constraints imposed upon creative expression by the conditions of war. It would seem that the uncertain events of 1939–45 induced in Larkin's writing a divergence away from direct statement and ideological commitment towards the kind of poetry favoured by Vernon Watkins and others: mellifluous, mystifying and resolutely apolitical. In a climate of international conflict, such poetry was 'safe' as well as fashionable. Larkin's own account of his meeting with Watkins (to whom he attributes the Yeatsian tendencies in *The North Ship*) emphasises this wartime context. Watkins, he explains, had visited the Oxford English Club in 1943, 'being stationed at an Air Force camp nearby', and after distributing volumes of Yeats' poetry had 'disappeared, exalted, into the blackout' (Larkin, 1983, p.29). It must be stressed that what Larkin and his generation were responding to was not the political rhetoric of 'Easter 1916' or 'Meditations in Time of Civil War', but 'the particularly potent music' that characterises the early lyrics of W.B. Yeats (Larkin, 1983, p.29). What was being fashioned here was a poetry of political quietism rather than political commitment, and this preference seems to have determined the composition and selection of poems in *The North Ship*. Prior to 1943, however, Larkin was writing a poetry that was much more in tune with the Auden group: a poetry that is often surprisingly outspoken, shrewdly observant and wittily ironic. If there are significant continuities between the earlier and the later poems, it is here that they begin.

What the publication of the *Collected Poems* also reveals is that the transition from *The North Ship* to *The Less Deceived* was by no means as smooth and straightforward as some critics have suggested. In fact, Larkin tried unsuccessfully to publish a typescript of poems completed in 1947, and many of these remained unpublished until 1988. Previous accounts of Larkin's poetic development based on simplified notions of literary influence are clearly untenable. To reassess the early part of Larkin's career it is necessary to look at three neglected areas of his work: the poems written between 1938 and 1944; those poems from *The North Ship* which appeared simultaneously in the anthology *Poetry from Oxford in Wartime* (1945); and the poems which constituted the unpublished typescript *In the Grip of Light* (1947).

One of the most intriguing of the early poems is a twenty-two stanza work in four sections, probably written shortly after the outbreak of war. The title, 'After-Dinner Remarks', seems curiously inappropriate in view of the poem's ostensibly serious and sombre subject matter, though it serves to establish a context in which private musings spill over into public address. Like the much later 'Vers de Société' the poem is a dramatisation of restricted choices in the face of inevitable 'failure and remorse'. There is a strong tendency towards introspection but this is repeatedly undercut by self-mockery:

> Pondering reflections as
>   Complex and deep as these
> I saw my life as in a glass:
> Set to music (negro jazz) . . .

                                    (p. 239)

What is most significant is that the poem's preoccupation with powerlessness and the failure to act is clearly related to the immediate events of war. The speaker's consciousness is shaped by the fear of imminent death:

> Choose what you can: I do remain
>   As neuter: and meanwhile
> Exploding shrapnel bursts the men
> Who thought perhaps they would disdain
> The world that from its reechy den
>   Emerges with a smile;
>
> All the familiar horrors we
>   Associate with others
> Are coming fast along our way:
> The wind is warning in our tree
> And morning papers still betray
>   The shrieking of the mothers.

                                    (p.241)

The use of 'neuter' rather than 'neutral' is in keeping with the poem's emphasis on sexual impotence. Throughout the early poems, the speaker's failure to establish fulfilling relationships is symptomatic of the more general sense of dissatisfaction and unfulfilment associated with wartime Britain. The imagery of military combat and the warning of impending 'horrors' are surprisingly explicit. In comparison, the later poems in *The North Ship* might well appear oblique and withdrawn.

The satirical idiom of 'After-Dinner Remarks' is characteristic of late 1930s poetry and recalls such well-known pieces as Auden's 'Song for the New Year' and C. Day Lewis's 'Newsreel'. What is most obvious here is the poem's exposure of a self-induced forgetfulness among the English middle class and the nervous, uneasy alignment of fear and frolic that keeps breaking through. With polite and incongruous diction, the poem invites its readers to escape from wartime realities into sensuous pleasures:

> And so, while summer on this day
>   Enacts her dress rehearsals,
> Let us forget who has to die,
> Swim in the delicious bay,
> Experience emotion by
>   The marvellous cathedrals . . .

(p.241)

'After-Dinner Remarks' is significant, not only because it so tellingly anticipates the dilemmas of will and choice in Larkin's later work, but because it intervenes so directly in contemporary political events. At the same time, it reveals the difficulties faced by a new generation of writers coming to maturity in the war years, particularly in reconciling private reflections and public fears. At this stage, the tension between withdrawal and commitment can be settled only by the dissolving imagery of night and sleep.

Images of night and darkness continue to evoke the uncertainties of wartime Britain, as is evident in 'Midsummer Night, 1940'. Like most of the early works, this poem is precise about its own wartime context and about the thoughts and feelings that emanate from that context. Again, it is worth stressing that these early poems are often more firmly located in place and time than those in *The North Ship*:

> The sun falls behind Wales; the towns and hills
> Sculptured on England, wait again for night
> As a deserted beach the tide that smoothes

> Its rimpled surface flat: as pale as moths
> Faces from factory pass home, for what respite
> Home offers: crowds vacate the public halls . . .
>
> (p.244)

The point of transition suggested by midsummer becomes the occasion for a sombre meditation on changing social attitudes and religious beliefs. The speaker shifts his attention from the factory workers of the present to 'other times, when heavy ploughmen snored, / And only some among the wealthy sneered'. Modern civilisation, in contrast, is free of superstition and legend, and yet seems unable to offer any lasting happiness or security. Enlightenment has its own painful disabilities, the speaker suggests, and in the absence of sustaining myths it seems much harder, not easier, to choose what is 'right'. Rationality is regarded here as 'a compulsory snare', a guarantee of pain. The image of angels yearning in an empty heaven issues from a troubled agnostic consciousness and anticipates some of the more strident expressions of disbelief in the later work. The title of the poem, however, reminds us that Larkin's agnosticism belongs to a particular historical moment and should not be seen in isolation from the general formation of attitudes and ideas in the years between 1939 and 1945. The point is reinforced by a poem written three years later: 'A Stone Church Damaged by a Bomb'. War, in this case, has inflicted a wound upon 'the petrified heart' of faith, and the speaker who once 'worshipped that whispering shell' wonders if the experience it held can ever be recreated (p.269). The speaker admires the building because it once seemed to defy and outstrip nature, and yet the organic imagery of the poem, especially the idea of religious experience as 'coral . . . set budding under seas', suggests that his main concern now is with the damaging effects of war on the tradition and continuity represented by the church.

Six months after 'Midsummer Night, 1940' Larkin composed 'Out in the lane I pause', a poem which makes similar use of a night-time setting to explore the anxieties and dilemmas of a society at war. Once again, that specific social context is conveyed with an impression of closely observed detail. The speaker watches the light gleaming from 'the little railway / That runs nearby', and hears the footsteps of 'Girls and their soldiers from the town' (p.253). The poem effectively dramatises the uncertainties of war by intimately relating the future of these lovers to the eventual outcome of the conflict: their 'wish for quiet days' must be held in abeyance and 'they must pursue their separate ways'. In a mood of sorrow the speaker asks 'If things are really what they seem', but the sky can only answer 'It is so'. The ending of a year adds an emotional charge to the poem, as it does in Thomas Hardy's 'The Darkling Thrush', and Larkin's conclusion is no more assured than Hardy's in its recognition that 'trust / Alone is best' (p.254). At the same time, the emotional turmoil which the poem seeks to clarify and resolve is clearly informed by its particular wartime context, and the experience of love and fulfilment indefinitely postponed begins to appear as a characteristic aspect of Larkin's work.

Other early poems such as 'Ultimatum' and 'Conscript' deal with the subject of war obliquely, though their titles have an obvious military significance. The predominant images are those of confinement and entrapment. It is clear that the fears and constraints of these early works are not those of some timeless 'human condition' but the immediate experiences of wartime Britain. 'Ultimatum' tells us that the ancient saying 'Life is yours' has been 'exploded' (p.243). A secure future can no longer be taken for granted, and decisions and choices are inevitably complicated and frustrated by war. Consequently, there is a need for vigilance and clear-sightedness, as the title of another poem, 'Observation', suggests. Here, the attitudes associated with books and dreams are firmly displaced as the speaker insists on emotional honesty and truthfulness. What is especially interesting about 'Observation' is not only its striking anticipation of *The Less Deceived*, but its provocative use of military imagery in a way that recalls some of the better known poetry of the late 1930s. If Hardy and Edward Thomas are echoed in 'Out in the lane I pause', it is undoubtedly W.H. Auden who provides the example for this politically overt style of writing. Larkin's reference to a 'government of medalled fears' is a sceptical response to the deceptive practice of 'putting on a brave face' in a time of crisis (p.264). 'Observation' was first published in the *Oxford University Labour Club Bulletin* in November 1941, and its final declaration that 'nothing can be found for poor men's fires' reveals a youthfully dissident and non-conformist side to Larkin's early work.

Perhaps the most ambitious of these early compositions, however, is 'New Year Poem', dated 31 December 1940. It seems a remarkably mature poem for the eighteen-year-old Larkin to have written.

The reference to 'this shattered city' in stanza three is a clear indication that the poem was prompted by the bombing of Coventry on 14 November 1940. A journey from Oxford to Coventry after the bombing provides Larkin with a crucial episode in his novel *Jill*. Until the publication of the *Collected Poems* it was commonly assumed that Larkin's poetry simply ignored the bombing, along with the rest of the war. Like the novel, however, 'New Year Poem' recreates a wartime setting where continuing normality prevails against sudden disruption, giving the city a strange and yet familiar appearance: houses are deserted and windows are smashed, and yet buses and bicycles still occupy the roads. As with *Jill*, the poem plays out a private, emotional drama in a devastated setting, and as with the lovers in 'Out in the lane I pause' the 'Eden that all wish to recreate' is brutally deferred. In the manner of Auden's 'Song for the New Year', the poem cautions its readers against harbouring dangerous illusions and fantasies: 'and all must take their warning / From these brief dreams of unsuccessful charms'. Like Auden's 'Song', Larkin's 'New Year Poem' approaches the festive midnight hour with irony and dismay, leaving the bells unrung and the bottle unopened. The syntax and vocabulary are unmistakably those of Auden: 'Tomorrow in the offices the year on the stamps will be altered; / Tomorrow new diaries consulted, new calendars stand . . .' (p.256). It is clear, then, that Larkin's emergence as a poet must be regarded in the context of war. We cannot account for Larkin's development as a writer simply in terms of the competing influences of Hardy and Yeats. These early poems are, of course, strongly derivative, but the most obvious model is the poetry of W.H. Auden and Louis MacNeice, which came to be regarded as the dominant literary discourse of the late 1930s and early 1940s.

As the war progressed, that discourse of the 1930s became much more difficult to sustain and Larkin resorted to the more obscure and introspective idiom of *The North Ship*. Like the work of his predecessors, Larkin's early poetry acknowledges that 'there is always a changing at the root, / And a real world in which time really passes' (p.255). Where Larkin's work departs most obviously from the poetry of the Auden generation is in its determination to recognise that 'world' and yet to abandon any attempt to change it. A slightly later poem beginning 'Time and Space were only their disguises' is also preoccupied with the bombing of Coventry and indicates how the war seems to rob the speaker of any volition, leaving him passive and helpless: 'But now this blackened city in the snow / Argues a will that cannot be my own' (p.260). After 1945 there is a gradual hardening of this stance, and what begins as disenchantment settles into an attitude of determined passivity and political quietism. A broad appraisal of Larkin's work between 1938 and 1945 suggests that the poems which were selected for publication in *The North Ship* were those which were most cautious and withdrawn in their attitudes to the war and therefore least controversial and least polemical.

Ten of the poems that were published in *The North Ship* also appeared in the anthology *Poetry from Oxford in Wartime* (1945). All were written between 1943 and 1944, and they mark a distinctive stage of development in Larkin's work. Larkin himself acknowledged the impact of Yeats after 1943, and this is certainly evident in these poems, but the determination to move into a new poetic mode is, nevertheless, motivated and informed by the circumstances of war. Critics have commented upon the Yeatsian music of 'All catches alight', but what is most significant about the poem is that it constitutes an elegy for the war dead. The refrain *'A drum taps: a wintry drum'* (recalling Walt Whitman's American Civil War poems in *Drum-Taps*) sets up the elegiac impulse (p.272). At the same time, the vibrant rhythm of the poem creates a shift of energy, while the imagery of spring is repeatedly given precedence over that of winter.

The same elegiac mood is evident in the second poem of the series, 'The moon is full tonight'. Here, there is a strong contrast between the moon, which is 'definite and bright', and the world of disturbance and doubts below. The poem acknowledges a diminished existence in which 'All quietness and certitude of worth' are 'gone from earth' (p.274). Again, however, there is an attempt to counter this mood of loss with a new sense of beginning, and the poem which follows – 'The horns of the morning' – acts as an emotional coda:

> The dawn reassembles,
> Like the clash of gold cymbals
> The sky spreads its vans out
> The sun hangs in view.

Even so, the outlook of these poems remains cautious and uncertain; the speaker inhabits a world where everything is 'frail and unsure' (p.275).

There is, throughout these wartime poems, a strong impression of frustrated love which is part of a deeper grieving over unfulfilled and unrealised ambitions. Prevalent images of 'running water' and 'straying winds' suggest a period of restless creativity, 'a season of unrest'. But there is also the idea of waiting for morning, and emerging from darkness signals both the end of war and the realisation of a poetic vocation. It is in keeping with later developments in Larkin's work (see, for instance, 'Waiting for breakfast') that 'poetic calling' should be realised not in the moment of love's fulfilment but in the moment of its denial. Two lines in 'Love, we must part now' serve to illustrate the prevailing mood of 1943–4: 'Never has sun more boldly paced the sky / Never were hearts more eager to be free' (p.290).

The appearance of ten poems from *The North Ship* in *Poetry from Oxford in Wartime* ought to remind us that *The North Ship* is, itself, a wartime collection of poems. The war is approached obliquely and with less immediacy than some of the uncollected poems of 1938–43, and yet it is undoubtedly a crucial shaping factor. Our understanding of the poetry remains incomplete, however, unless we take into consideration the unpublished typescript, *In the Grip of Light*, which Larkin prepared for publication between *The North Ship* and *The Less Deceived*. The projected arrangement of poems for *In the Grip of Light* (see pp.317–18) provides an extremely interesting insight into Larkin's work between 1943 and 1947. It includes six poems which had already been published in *The North Ship* and two which were to appear later in *The Less Deceived*, but the other sixteen poems were not generally available until the publication of *Collected Poems*.

All the poems in *The North Ship* had been completed by October 1944. *In the Grip of Light*, however, consists mainly of poems which coincide with the ending of war and overlap with the early years of post-war reconstruction. Larkin considered *In the Grip of Light* to have been a 'portentous' title for his projected book, but in the context of post-war Britain it proves to be both apt and revealing. Social historians have shown how the coming of peace was identified in the popular consciousness as 'a new dawn', and how, in the event, the return to 'normality' proved slow and protractive. Arthur Marwick, for instance, claims that between 1945 and 1950 'the country lay in a crepuscular zone with the shadows of night as firm upon the landscape as the heartening hints of the rising sun'

(Marwick, 1986, p.22). This idea of a 'crepuscular zone' is clearly evident in Larkin's poems of the period, with their twilight reflections, their cold dawn landscapes and their unsettled feelings of despair and anticipation.

'Winter' and 'Night-Music', both of which had previously appeared in *The North Ship*, envisage a deathly landscape where 'shrivelled men' lie buried, and yet in the elegiac mode of 'All catches alight' they seek a miraculous transformation of the dead. 'Night-Music' ends with the stars singing through the night: 'Blow bright, blow bright / The coal of this unquickened world' (p.300). Both poems belong to the period 1943–4. In May 1945, however, the war was over, and in 'Lift through the breaking day' (one of the first poems written after the end of the war) there is an ecstatic sense of release and affirmation:

> Fly on towards the sea:
>   Sing there upon the beach
> Till all's beyond death's reach,
> And empty shells reply
>   That all things flourish.
>
> (p.308)

'Lift through the breaking day' catches the buoyant national spirit and popular resolve that followed the celebrated election of the Labour Party to government in 1945. There is rarely anything so affirmative in the poems written after that date.

The idealism of 1945 was short-lived and the new government was to face a problematic period of post-war reconstruction. If the title *In the Grip of Light* aptly describes the 'crepuscular' nature of this period, it also describes the uneasy emergence of Larkin's poetic imagination and further hints at a crisis of religious belief. These moments of private and public change are, of course, intricately related. The war had inflicted severe damage on traditional religious observance, and in the poems written by Larkin in 1946 there is evidence of a profound and troubled agnosticism. 'Going', written early in 1946 and placed at the beginning of *Collected Poems*, provides a clear indication of the direction in which the mature poetry was to develop. As its original title – 'Dying Day' – suggests, the subject of the poem is death and its attendant loss of consciousness, but the existential problems which the poem raises are undoubtedly related to the events of the preceding years. The poem is one of a number of ontological riddles in Larkin's work (see 'Days', for example), and in a seemingly direct and simple way it raises questions about knowledge and perception. 'Going', in this sense, constitutes a negative image or denial of 'being'.

Another poem from 1946, 'And the wave sings because it is moving', makes the connection between private and public concerns apparent when it speaks of the heart's 'skill / In surviving' (p.6). 'How to exist' or 'how to survive' is the fundamental question which these poems of the immediate post-war years address. The dilemma persists and it finds its consummate expression in the affirmative, but nevertheless guarded, conclusion to 'An Arundel Tomb': 'What will survive of us is love' (p.111). A troubled agnostic consciousness is evident in the persistent twilight imagery, but also in the lingering religious vocabulary of poems like 'Come then to prayers' or 'To a Very Slow Air', though this vocabulary is emptied of its usual associations. 'The Dedicated', for instance, ends with 'the colder advent, / The quenching of candles'. As Roger Day has argued, many of Larkin's poems take the form of 'secular hymns' and continue to draw on a traditional religious vocabulary of prayer and praise (Day, 1989, p.88).

Larkin's agnostic attitudes determine the way in which sexual relationships are regarded in the early poems. Nearly always, love is treated with caution and ambivalence as if, like religion, it commits us to a ritual which might promise to 'solve and satisfy' but might also prove false. The most striking instance of these attitudes can be found in 'Wedding-Wind', where the transition from 'the night of the high wind' to 'this perpetual morning' once again typifies the predominant strand of imagery in these post-war poems. The compound noun of the title establishes a correspondence between the regenerative, creative power of the wind and sexual consummation. The wedding night is a moment of unique happiness, but the anxious questions of the second stanza imply a measure of doubt about whether such happiness can be sustained. The new-found delight of the bride seems to offer hope and resilience, and a way of contemplating 'even death', but the poem nevertheless ends with a question mark (p.11). In the context of the wedding, the imagery of wind and water seems to carry a spiritual, sacramental power, but the poem turns on whether these are providential or purely arbitrary forces. There are several references to 'kneeling' in the early poems, but 'kneeling as cattle' suggests an action based on instinct rather than a gesture of prayer and thankfulness.

'Wedding-Wind' was written in 1946 and its heralding of 'perpetual morning' is in keeping with the powerful sense of release that accompanies Larkin's immediate post-war writing. What is also evident, though, is that the ending of the war coincided with a crisis of belief in Larkin's work and a deep uncertainty about the 'vocation' of the poet in modern society. Larkin's emergence as a mature writer must be seen within the complex formative period of the war years, and much more attention than usual must be given to the work written before the publication of *The North Ship* in 1945. As Peter Porter commented in his review of Larkin's *Collected Poems*, the early work is 'not juvenilia in the usual sense', but a series of Audenesque variations which are 'prodigiously accomplished'. There is no doubt in Porter's mind that 'the stuff which got into *The North Ship* is inferior to what came before it' (Porter, 1988). It is clear now that Larkin's response to the work of Auden and his contemporaries was not one of rejection but one of careful modification within the context of war, and the persistence of this influence can be detected in poems as late as those of *High Windows* (1974). The insecurities of wartime Britain helped to shape a poetry of restricted choices, quietistic moods and disappointed ideals, but in a more positive way produced a poetry of tenacious survival and vigilant awareness.

Fables of Freedom: *The Less Deceived*

The 'victory' of 1945 was a celebration of freedom, but it was also a decisive moment in the history of Britain's decline as a world power. With the economic structure of its former 'greatness' severely shaken, with its physical and human resources massively depleted, and with its foreign policy heavily overshadowed by the actions of the United States and the Soviet Union, Britain could no longer sustain its role as a leading imperial nation. As Correlli Barnett has argued in *The Collapse of British Power*, the nation 'emerged into the post-war era with the foundations of her former independent national power as completely destroyed as those of France or Germany, but with the extra and calamitous drawback that, as a "victor", she failed to realise it'. British power had 'quietly vanished amid the stupendous events of the Second World War' (Barnett, 1972, p.593). If the notion of victory was in some ways an illusion, so too was the glorious promise of 'a world fit to live in', one of many slogans that accompanied the euphoric election of the Labour Party to office in 1945.

The new government did, of course, carry through a radical programme of reforms, establishing a free and universal health service, an improved social security system, including insurance against unemployment and sickness, a free system of compulsory education and a comprehensive review of housing. By 1949 it was accepted that Britain was 'a Welfare State', and the term was one of approval rather than denigration. The necessary reforms were enabled by a spirit of agreement or consent among political parties, though this 'consensus' became much more difficult to maintain in the 1950s. The divergence of interests was apparent in the 1950 General Election, when the Conservatives reminded the electorate that the post-war years had been characterised by continued rationing, general drabness and restrictive economic policies. While the Labour Party campaigned in the spirit of 'Fair Shares For All', the Conservative Party promised 'to set the people free'. What constituted freedom was clearly a matter of debate. Aneurin Bevan had stated the position of the Labour Party firmly enough in 1945: 'Freedom for the worker means freedom from poverty, insecurity and unemployment. Freedom for the Tory means freedom of action to exploit the workers delivered into his hands by these' (Sinfield, 1989, p.89). In the event, the Labour government was returned with a much-reduced majority in 1950, only to be ousted from power a year later.

It was in 1951 that Philip Larkin published a small collection of poems with the title *XX Poems*, most of which were to appear in a later volume, *The Less Deceived* (1955). These poems belong to the period of post-war settlement in that they constitute a reappraisal and reconstruction of what had previously been regarded as 'traditional' values and ideals, including attitudes to work, religion and marriage. Stylistically they partake of the post-war social consensus in that they seek to combine a traditional poetic lyricism with a distinctively colloquial and contemporary idiom that derives from a lower-middle and working-class speech community. We find in the poems of *The Less Deceived* a careful and fastidious working out of an individual code of values consonant with the idea of 'personal freedom'. The response of the poems to the political reforms of 1945–51 is generally in keeping with that of the middle-class intelligentsia which tended to treat the new egalitarian spirit with caution and restraint. The tone of Larkin's poems in this period is characteristically defensive. 'Happiness' appears several times, but the word is invariably qualified. Significantly, the poem written to celebrate the birth of Sally Amis guards against the naïvety and idealism popularly associated with its title ('Born Yesterday') and wishes the child, among other things, a *vigilant* 'catching of happiness' (p.84). Vigilance, alertness and wariness define a particular set of attitudes and responses in post-war society and help us to understand what some critics have described as the 'limitations' in Larkin's poetry. As Alun Jones argued many years ago, the early poetry of Philip Larkin might be regarded as an expression of 'the sensitive and intelligent mind's refusal to be taken in' (Jones, 1962, p.147). In this context, to commit oneself through word or gesture, to bind oneself to any statement or positive attitude, is to risk losing one's 'freedom'. This conception of freedom is not the ideal of social democracy that many people hoped for after the war, but the persistent and beleaguered liberalism of an earlier generation in which the concerns and aspirations of 'the individual' (as distinct from 'society') are of paramount importance. So belittled and embattled is this idea of freedom that it sometimes amounts to little more than a freedom from illusion.

The title of *The Less Deceived* is an inversion of Ophelia's remark to Hamlet (III.i) that 'I was the more deceived'. In the context of post-war Britain, however, its cultural significance is far reaching. In a letter written to his publisher, George Hartley, in April 1955, Larkin explained that he had deliberately avoided a title 'that made any claims to policy or belief' and also referred to the 'sad-eyed (and clear-eyed) realism' that informed his work. Such an outlook was a product, he thought, of a 'fundamentally passive attitude to poetry (and life too . . .)' (Hartley, 1988, p.299). The combination of 'sad-eyed' and 'clear-eyed' is interesting, since it implies a measure of disenchantment and lost idealism but also a corresponding (and perhaps compensatory) determination to approach life in a rational and logical way. Such an approach is evident in those poems which explore modern attitudes to such things as work, leisure, love and death, but it is evident, too, in Larkin's philosophical preoccupation with questions of belief, knowledge and perception. All of these concerns were precipitated and intensified by the conditions of post-war reconstruction, and at a fundamental level many of the poems seem to be asking: 'What can we now trust?' or 'What can we now believe in?'

An extremely important influence in the immediate post-war period was Alfred Ayer's *Language, Truth and Logic*, published in a highly popular second edition in 1946. Central to Ayer's book is the idea that the verification of any proposition rests largely on 'some possible sense-experience' being relevant to the determination of its truth or falsehood. Ayer insisted upon the 'fruitlessness of attempting to transcend the limits of possible sense-experience' (Ayer, 1960, p.35). One of the key passages in *Language, Truth and Logic* has an immediate bearing on the substance and meaning of *The Less Deceived*:

> It must, of course, be admitted that our senses do sometimes deceive us . . . We say that the senses sometimes deceive us, just because the expectations to which our sense-experiences give rise do not always accord with what we subsequently experience. (Ayer, 1960, p.39)

It is precisely this suggestion that shapes the presentation of the male protagonist in the title poem, 'Deceptions'. In a more general way, though, the attempted 'verification' of experiences and propositions is a recurring impulse throughout *The Less Deceived*. While it would be unwise to regard Larkin's poetry as strictly 'empirical' (the term is problematical in *any* discussion of poetic technique), it would seem to be the case that Ayer's work (and the tradition of logical positivism from which it derived) gave to Larkin and his generation a welcome philosophical support for a literature that espoused the need for caution and scepticism. What has been identified as the 'empiricism' of the Movement operates in Larkin's poetry as a concern with seeing things clearly and truthfully. This tendency, however, had important political as well as philosophical implications, since it was essentially part of the more general revaluation of beliefs and values in post-war Britain.

To read *The Less Deceived* historically is to engage with a political context that ranges from Empire to Welfare State, from what was idealised as a 'glorious' colonial past to what was increasingly seen as an austere and mediocre domestic present. This perceived loss of power manifests itself in the wistful melancholy and elegiac lyricism of the poems, and it helps us to understand Larkin's 'sad-eyed' realism. Despite the determination of the poems to occupy themselves with the needs of the present, there are always those images of the past that 'lacerate / Simply by being over' (p.72). Tom Paulin has given an excellent account of how an early and little-known poem by Larkin, 'The March Past', embodies a deeply felt nationalist and imperialist sentiment (Paulin, 1990, p.779). Listening to the music of a military band, the speaker in the poem confesses 'a blind / Astonishing remorse for things now ended' (p.55).

Blake Morrison argues that patriotic emotion in the post-war years was more likely to be subdued than openly fervent and that such emotion usually operated in a form that would not appear obtrusive or offensive. He claims that the reason Larkin's 'At Grass' became one of the most popular post-war poems is that 'by allowing the horses to symbolize loss of power, Larkin manages to tap nostalgia for a past "glory that was England"' (Morrison, 1980, p.82). For this reason, he identifies 'At Grass' as 'a poem of post-imperial *tristesse*'. Philip Hobsbaum complains that 'such an interpretation . . . rests on an assumed prose sense' (Hobsbaum, 1988, p.286), but this is certainly not the case, since Morrison pays careful attention to the subtle linguistic contrasts of the poem and also makes the very pertinent remark that the intense feeling of the poem is 'more than an emotion about racehorses in old age' (Morrison, 1980, p.84).

Tom Paulin agrees with Morrison that Larkin's 'sad lyricism is rooted in a culture' and that what it frequently evokes is 'a sense of diminished purpose and fading imperial power' (Paulin, 1990, p.779). He sees the horses in 'At Grass' as emblems of a lost heroism and a lost social order. What supports this argument is the indication in the manuscript drafts of the poem that the fifth line of stanza two initially read 'Medallioned with gratitude'. The suggestion here is that the Second World War is part of the poem's immediate social context, a point that seems to be reinforced by the word 'Squadrons' which is usually associated with military formations (p.29). 'Fifteen years ago' effectively places the poem's focus of interest in that moment of assured greatness just before the outbreak of war. The manuscript drafts show that the line originally began 'Through thirty-three and -four'. The poem is quite careful, then, in locating its moment of lost glory in the years preceding the international crisis that led to war.

'At Grass' is a quintessentially English poem. Its Englishness is evident not just in its memories of 'Cups and Stakes and Handicaps' and its bright evocations of 'classic' summers, but also in its modified use of the pastoral convention. There are hints of eighteenth-century English pastoralism in the elegiac mood of the poem, but Larkin's version of pastoral is one that has been adapted to the particular needs of post-war society; its pastures are a place of 'shelter', a place fittingly described by the negative prefix in 'unmolesting meadows'. 'At Grass' is a powerfully evocative poem which draws skilfully on the traditional resources of English lyricism. Its deployment of familiar stylistic devices is evident in the alliterative echoes of 'shade' and 'shelter' or 'crowds' and 'cries'; in the verbal suggestiveness of 'distresses' and 'brims' or the delicate adjectival shading of 'faint' and 'faded'; it is evident, too, in the hanging 'cry' of stanza three or the poignant, hesitant slippage between the penultimate and the final stanzas, and in the dying fall of the closing line, with its delicate, archaic inversion. If we compare the early manuscript reference to 'tinted pictures on the walls' with 'inlay faded, classic Junes', we can detect the kind of compression and suggestiveness that the poem's vocabulary is seeking to capture. It is not difficult to understand why the poem has been such a popular success in practical criticism classes. There is an elegant formality in the stanzaic and rhythmic structure of the poem, but there is also an appealing conversational level in the casual 'perhaps' and in the wistful question: 'Do memories plague their ears like flies?' These devices are a source of linguistic pleasure, but they are also rhetorical ploys which invite us to give our assent to a particular version of English culture. The degree of lexical cohesion evident in the collocation of 'fable', 'faint' and 'faded', or in the repetition of 'summer by summer', is both strategic and effective. The poem imparts a certain perspective, a certain way of regarding experience, and seeks to persuade us of its validity. 'At Grass' reveals the way in which great achievements are 'fabled' in memory, but we should not overlook the fact that it is, itself, a kind of fable. Like several poems in *The Less Deceived*, 'At Grass' is a fable of freedom.

Cox and Dyson, in their clear and informative practical criticism of 'At Grass', claim that Larkin's horses 'have a freedom which humans can never achieve' and they also point, significantly, to the 'almost quietistic mood' of the final stanza. They prefer, however, to interpret the poem in a universal sense, in terms of 'the inevitability of fate' (Cox and Dyson, 1963, pp.140–1). The weakness of such an argument is that the notion of ideal freedom is difficult to maintain in view of the rather muted ending of the poem. In the context of post-war society, however, the poem's ambiguous sense of release is readily understandable and entirely in keeping with the complex and uncertain debate about 'freedom' in those years. The assumption that the horses gallop 'for what *must* be joy' (italics added) is, like many of Larkin's assertions about fulfilment, an insecure realisation of happiness. The 'bridles' of the closing stanza are a more appropriate image of Welfare State dependency than of 'ideal freedom'. While mourning the lost splendour of 'heat, / And littered grass', the poem refuses to acknowledge any ideal state of freedom and settles instead for a quietly subdued and passive outlook.

A similar concern about freedom and a similar use of the animal fable can be found in 'Wires'. Just as 'At Grass' is more than a poem about retired racehorses, so 'Wires' is clearly something other than a statement about the effective control of cattle. The vague attractions of 'anywhere' and the equally unspecific and curious use of 'Beyond the wires' to name the desired state of freedom suggest that the poem is operating at the level of allegory or parable (p.48). The repetition of 'wires' draws our attention to the way in which the poem's rhyme scheme sets up a pattern of internal reflection – abcd dcba – thereby reinforcing a preoccupation with containment and enclosure. The shift from 'widest prairies' in the opening line to 'widest senses' in the closing line encourages the idea that freedom is an imaginary condition with no material existence. The familiar quatrains and loose iambic lines convey a sense of authoritative wisdom, so that the poem takes on the appearance of a well-established proverb or fable. What we might easily overlook is that the fable works to 'naturalise' the conditions of restraint that it describes. Freedom ceases to be seen as a social and historical provision and comes to be regarded (note the effect of 'blunder' and 'violence') as a dangerous illusion. An effective criticism of the poem should not rest in admiration of its apparent timeless human wisdom but should seek to explain how its language renders a particular 'way of seeing' and how its ideas are shaped by a particular social context.

'Myxomatosis' is another animal fable, no doubt inspired by the outbreak of rabbit disease in Kent and Sussex in October 1953. This time, the poem signals its allegorical function by imagining the rabbit asking 'What trap is this? Where were its teeth concealed?'

(p.100). The speaker's reflections further suggest that the poem is establishing a parallel between the fate of the animal and a certain dimension of human existence. The words 'caught', 'trap' and 'jaws' suggest that the common experience being described is one of suffering, powerlessness and helplessness. The final statement, 'You may have thought things would come right again / If you could only keep quite still and wait', exudes compassion, but at the level of allegory it also registers a deeply sceptical outlook. The poem appears to function so 'naturally' that the world view which informs it is easily overlooked.

Several poems in *The Less Deceived* show an implied sense of resentment at the limitations of contemporary social experience and some even initiate a spirited, though ultimately futile, rebellion. 'Toads' and 'Poetry of Departures' belong in this category. With 'Toads', however, the element of fable once again conditions the kind of enquiry about freedom that takes place, and the immediate substitution of 'toad' for 'work' in the opening line invites us to consider the idea of work as something unappealing but nevertheless 'natural'. Consequently, the poem never directly considers the idea of work as a socially constructed activity. Even so, it is a poem that emerges from a familiar post-war context, and in its anxiety about 'work' it shares a fundamental concern with a great deal of 1950s literature, including the fiction and drama of the period. In Shelagh Delaney's play *A Taste of Honey* (1956), for instance, a working-class mother tells her daughter: 'There's two w's in your future. Work or want ...' (Delaney, 1987, p.29). Both words carry significance in Larkin's poetry, and 'Toads' is a good example of a familiar and recurring debate about individual rights and responsibilities in a modern democratic society. Although it seems to evade the ultimate questions of how and why work or labour is organised, 'Toads' is extremely interesting and valuable in terms of the language and form through which it registers changing and conflicting social attitudes. It is this relationship between textual structure and social structure that proves most revealing.

Most poems can be read not just as propositions about events but as acts of speech. 'Toads' calls attention to itself as *utterance* and in doing so the poem demonstrates one of the most innovative and culturally significant aspects of Larkin's work, which is its sustained and counterpointed use of vernacular English within traditional lyric forms. The opening stanza of 'Toads' consists of two abrupt questions, the first of which is a rush of monosyllables:

Why should I let the toad *work*
Squat on my life?
Can't I use my wit as a pitchfork
And drive the brute off?

(p.89)

From the outset we are given a strong impression of a speaking voice. The language is vigorous and colloquial, and the shifts and stresses of the speaker's tonal gestures are indicated typographically in the italicised forms of certain words and phrases: *work, starves, Stuff your pension!* Syntactically, as well, the poem takes the form of an argument, with conjunctions and exclamations providing the necessary cohesion and linkage: (Ah . . . But . . . For . . . And). The verbal mood and tense of the poem shift from the interrogative first stanza to the indicative middle stanzas (where declaration and statement take over from question) and then to the subjunctive and imaginary 'Ah, were I courageous enough . . .' The poem is written in rhyming quatrains, but the lines are short and brisk and the rhymes are approximate (soils/bills), so that the impression of actual speech is maintained throughout. The obvious repetition of 'Lots of folk live' also contributes to this effect. The context of speech or 'utterance' is reinforced by the closing lines, where a typical rhetorical ploy – that of antithesis – is brought into play: 'I don't *say* . . . But I do *say*' (italics added).

We can see, then, how poetry might be regarded as *social discourse*. The voice of the poem strives to occupy a neutral or 'average' position but it can only do so by defining itself as different or separate from other social classes and categories: from those who 'live on their wits' and from those who 'live up lanes / With fires in a bucket'. The ludicrous alliteration of 'Lecturers, lispers, / Losels, loblolly-men, louts' conveys an exaggerated sense of derision, but it also suggests how social 'types' are arbitrarily classified ('losels' are rakes or profligates, 'loblolly-men' are surgeons' mates on ship). From a sociolinguistic perspective, it can be seen how the poem draws on a broad range of speech forms to convey an effect of impartiality and yet cannot do so without hinting at the extent of division and difference within its social context. 'Skinny as whippets', for instance, belongs to a working-class speech community, while 'unspeakable wives', the subject of this endearing comparison, typifies the polite condescension of middle-class English. Similarly, the word 'stuff' appears both in the vernacular 'Stuff your pension' and in the more scholarly 'that's the stuff / That dreams are made on', with its overt reference to Shakespeare's *The Tempest* (IV.i). These observations help us to relate the poem to its social and cultural context. The language of 'Toads' (including the language of popular cliché: 'The fame and the girl and the money') is clearly in keeping with the democratising tendencies of post-war Britain, and it directs itself to a broad and changing community of readers. As Roland Barthes has argued, the modern writer's search for 'a spoken level of writing' can be equated with 'the anticipation of a homogeneous social state' (Barthes, 1967, p.93). The range and flexibility of Larkin's vernacular idiom represents a significant realignment and readjustment in the language of English poetry.

In keeping with its broad sociolinguistic range, 'Toads' very deftly embraces both conformism and non-conformism; it begins in a mood of rebellion and defiance and ends in a mood of quietism and apparent resignation. This is not to say that the speaker's position is, after all, one of simple neutrality. The closing lines of the poem with their considered weighing of attitudes and their contemplation of 'spiritual truth' signal the poem's allegiance to a specific tradition of English intellectual life already alluded to in this study. The preponderance of personal pronouns – 'Why should *I* . . . were *I* . . . squats in *me* . . . will never allow *me*' – are an indication of a stubborn liberal individualism which continues to regard the essential idea of freedom in terms of the individual *against* society. Any notion of rebelling against the system, then, is personalised and consequently doomed to failure. The closing stanza is blatantly equivocal, insisting that while the physical nature of work does not necessarily justify the appeal of an imaginary release, it cannot altogether do without it. In the end, the two attitudes to work – commitment and escape – are presented not so much as alternatives as mutually dependent ideals. By setting up what appear to be alternatives and then surreptitiously cancelling them out, the poem effectively maintains its liberal-minded commitment to the status quo. The final effect of the poem's antithetical structure – 'one – other / bodies – spiritual / either – both' – is to mystify rather than clarify the issues at stake.

The uncertain reference to 'spiritual truth' in 'Toads' is a reminder that Larkin's political liberalism is closely related to an increasingly widespread agnosticism in the post-war years. Both are

forms of belief or disbelief which manifest themselves in ambivalent
linguistic structures. The punning title of 'Church Going', for instance,
testifies to both the erosion of 'the Church' as an institution and to
the persistence of some kind of ritual observance. As with 'Toads',
the speaker of the poem responds to conflicting attitudes and also
draws on a variety of speech forms; he is 'bored' and 'uninformed' –
as we see in his casual reference to 'some brass and stuff / Up at the
holy end' – and yet he appears to be knowledgeable and articulate
about such things as 'parchment, plate and pyx' (p.97). This
apparent contradiction reveals how Larkin's speakers are 'constructed' in a way that allows the poem to explore different
perceptions of the same event (the technique is less obtrusive in the
case of 'The Whitsun Weddings'). The final paragraph expands the
poem's observations by making the experiences of its persona
generally representative: 'A serious house on serious earth it is, / In
whose blent air all our compulsions meet, / Are recognised and
robed as destinies. / And that much never can be obsolete...'
(p.98). The subtle movement from the first person singular to the
first person plural, 'we' or 'our', is a characteristic device in Larkin's
poetry and one that is predicated upon the assent of its readers. In
this way, the poem is able to accommodate both a sceptical view of
religious ritual ('robed as destinies' suggests an act of 'make-
believe') and an assertion of the continuing value and significance of
those rituals. Even so, the question of 'what remains when disbelief
is gone' is an indication of how radical and unsettling the agnosticism in Larkin's poems can be.

'Church Going' was written in 1954 and an essential aspect of its
social context is the marked and general decline in religious
attendance after 1945. Arthur Marwick claims that at the beginning
of 1950 less than 10 per cent of the population were churchgoers.
'Church Going' embodies what Marwick calls 'secular Anglican-
ism': it concedes that 'belief must die' and yet it cannot relinquish
the spirit of tradition that the Church of England represents
(Marwick, 1986, p.16). As the Church seemed to lose its importance
in matters of education and welfare, there were fears that its place in
modern society would become marginal. 'Church Going' acknowledges those fears and reveals its own specific context by locating
'this cross of ground' at the edge of 'suburb scrub'. The relationship
between Larkin's agnosticism and the political quietism already
alluded to becomes evident if we place Larkin's poem in the broader

international context of the post-war years. Edwin Morgan suggests an illuminating contrast between 'Church Going' and 'The Partisans' Graves' by the Russian poet Yevgeny Yevtushenko, pointing out how Larkin's phrase 'so many dead' seems to betray a lack of interest in who these people were and what they lived and died for. He finds in Larkin's poem a characteristic 'distancing and dissolving of conflict . . . a fear of statement and commitment' (Morgan, 1961, p.4).

One of the consequences of the shift in the post-war years towards a more secular society was that the 'transcendent' significance previously embodied in the Church was transferred to an ideal of 'the Self'. The problems of existence which the Church had regarded as its proper sphere of concern became, for many people, a matter of private and personal resolve. Jonathan Dollimore has argued that in the post-war era, 'salvation comes, typically, to be located in the pseudo-religious absolute of Personal Integrity' (Dollimore, 1984, p.268). This 'personal integrity' is, of course, fundamental to the idea of being 'less deceived', and it provides the motivating impulse behind such poems as 'Toads' and 'Poetry of Departures'. In 'Arrivals, Departures', freedom is defined in terms of the crucial choices which the traveller has to make. 'Never knowing' the eventual outcome of those choices makes 'happiness' in this poem a tentative and provisional state (p.65). When the ideal of personal integrity breaks down, nihilism and negation threaten to take over. Alan Sinfield sees this tendency as a further consequence of post-war change: 'Distress at the fracturing of an older, stable social order which is felt to be necessary to civilization stimulates the move towards renunciation, transcending a world that seems now to offer so little' (Sinfield, 1983, p.88). The spirit of renunciation and transcendence seems to inform Larkin's 'Absences', with its contemplation of utter abandonment: 'Such attics cleared of me! Such absences!' (p.49). In 'Wants', the familiar rituals of existence – parties, sexual relationships, family gatherings – are displaced by powerful personal impulses 'beyond' and 'beneath' them. The idea of fulfilment usually associated with the word 'wants' is countered by another deep-seated 'desire': 'Beneath it all, desire of oblivion runs' (p.42).

A number of poems in *The Less Deceived* might be more appropriately described as 'existential' than 'empirical', in the sense that they are fundamentally concerned with ways of contemplating death, destiny, contingency and nothingness. 'Next, Please', for instance, might well be read in terms of the existentialist dictum that 'Human life in its entirety is life facing death' (Walsh, 1985, p.537). Such an approach must proceed with caution, for what is sometimes apparent is 'not a distinctive world view, or an existential stance, but a hesitancy to adopt one, to bring one's conflicts into resolution' (Brown, 1980, p.1). A very helpful clarification of this uncertain relationship between Larkin's poetry and modern philosophy can be found in Richard Rorty's *Contingency, irony, and solidarity*. Rorty explains the 'fear of dying' or 'fear of extinction' in Larkin's work in terms of an imagined loss of selfhood or erasure of one's own distinctiveness.

Focusing very effectively on the early poem 'Continuing to Live' (written just before the publication of *The Less Deceived* but not included in the book), Rorty claims that Larkin is concerned with private fulfilment but also with human solidarity. The poem's attempt to identify 'the blind impress / All our behavings bear' (p.94) involves *both* the particular contingencies or chance occurrences which make each of us 'I' *and* a concern with community or common humanity. The closing lines of the poem suggest that Larkin is reluctant to confine his sense of 'existence' to the thoughts of 'one man once, / And that one dying'. Rorty argues that the poem owes its interest and its strength to the tension between selfhood and solidarity, between the resigned acceptance of 'contingency' and the effort to transcend it. The argument retains its relevance when applied to later poems such as 'Mr Bleaney' and 'The Whitsun Weddings'. In Rorty's view, Larkin's existential stance might be defined as that of the *liberal ironist*: 'the sort of person who faces up to the contingency of his or her own most central beliefs and desires' but continues to find some consolation in the idea that other people are 'fellow sufferers' (Rorty, 1989, pp.xv, 23–7).

Rorty's remarks about the 'fear of extinction' in 'Continuing to Live' are clearly relevant to many of Larkin's better-known poems. Like 'Continuing to Live', 'Next, Please' powerfully renders the dramatic shock of existential experience as it breaks through all our habitual attempts to conceal the spectre of death. It is only in this ultimate confrontation, the poem implies, that we can free ourselves of illusion. What characterises the poem and serves to mitigate the sense of dread usually associated with existentialist writing is its familiar colloquial voice. 'Next, Please' employs many of the rhetorical devices already mentioned in the discussion of 'Toads'. The title, 'Next, Please', is a piece of black comedy and the poem's dominant image – a ship – is based on a popular and well-established proverb. Just as 'Wires' builds on the wisdom that 'the grass is always greener on the other side', so 'Next, Please' examines the claim that 'one day your ship will come in'. The prominent placing of the plural pronoun 'we' at the end of the opening line sets up a sense of shared expectancy which is reiterated in the emphatic 'every day / *Till then* we say'. This impression of actual speech is further conveyed in the exclamation of stanza two: 'How slow they are!'. The chiming syllables and diminished effect of each quatrain set up an appropriate tension between fulfilment and denial. The rhymes are sometimes comic and facile – 'stalks / balks', 'tits / it's' – but the final two stanzas possess a more sombre mood. The caesura and the rapid enjambment of the penultimate line have a decisive and clinching finality. The clash of popular wisdom and intellectual scrutiny, along with the sudden shift from colloquial banter to sombre meditation, gives 'Next, Please' its *frisson* of unease:

> We think each one will heave to and unload
> All good into our lives, all we are owed
> For waiting so devoutly and so long.
> But we are wrong:
>
> Only one ship is seeking us, a black-
> Sailed unfamiliar, towing at her back
> A huge and birdless silence. In her wake
> No waters breed or break.

> (p.52)

'Next, Please' might appear to be written from a bleaker philosophical position than 'Wires' or 'Toads', and its final stanza might well be reminiscent of the work of French symbolist poets, but its stylistic features are generally consistent with other poems in *The Less Deceived* and so, too, is its conception of freedom. Freedom, in this instance, is freedom from illusion, the freedom of individual awareness. Merle Brown is careful to dissociate Larkin's poems from 'the fearfulness of nihilism or existentialistic absurdity', and yet arrives at a similar conclusion about the kind of freedom the poems envisage: 'That freedom entails a recognition that one cannot rely on anything outside [oneself] as an origin, as a source of value' (Brown, 1980, pp.75, 77). Brown perhaps underestimates the sense of human solidarity which Richard Rorty emphasises (and which is evident in the plural pronouns of 'Next, Please'). Nevertheless, it is fair to say that the concept of freedom in these early poems is narrowly circumscribed. It might be argued further that the existential concerns of such poems as 'Next, Please' are closely attuned to the widespread spiritual and political quietism of the post-war years and need to be understood within that context.

It is not surprising, in view of the sustained debate about freedom after 1945, that so many of Larkin's poems should carefully weigh a desire for escape and release with a dutiful commitment to the status quo. Perhaps the most obvious example is 'Poetry of Departures':

> Sometimes you hear, fifth-hand,
> As epitaph:
> *He chucked up everything*
> *And just cleared off,*
> And always the voice will sound
> Certain you approve
> This audacious, purifying,
> Elemental move.

(p.85)

The casual 'fifth-hand' report of the opening lines and the shift from 'you' and 'he' to 'I' and 'we' in the second stanza create a linguistic structure that is *interpersonal*: it brings into collision a range of speech forms and their associated social attitudes. The poem is both formal and colloquial, cutting across class lines in its appeal to what we all know and experience: 'We all hate home / And having to be there'. The clichéd appearance of lines like *'He walked out on the whole crowd'* render the poem accessible and familiar. What is curious, though, is that the speaker moves from the apparent disapproval registered in the politely dismissive close of stanza one to a tentative identification with the purveyors of cliché: 'And they are right, I think'. By the final stanza, the poem has succeeded in neutralising the popular declaration of personal freedom or escape, not by refuting it but by accommodating it. Paradoxically, it is the imagined existence of an alternative way of life that helps the speaker to *stay* 'Sober and industrious'. By conducting its enquiry at the level of cliché and gossip – 'Surely I can, if he did?' – the poem appears to engage in a democratic way with 'popular' sentiment, but it also avoids the more rigorous debate that 'freedom' deserves.

In an excellent discussion of 'Poetry of Departures', Graham Holderness makes the point that there is a significant link between Larkin's resigned outlook and his acceptance of 'the common language' as an appropriate poetic idiom. The poem's commitment to 'a simple, no-nonsense diction' is such that any tendency to escape is inevitably treated as a 'superficial fantasy or fable' (see Cookson and Loughrey, 1989, p.109). One of the disadvantages of Larkin's easy colloquial banter is that it restricts the vision of the poem to the attitudes and values that such language embodies. What Holderness is criticising here is the poem's array of familiar assumptions and its passive acceptance of 'the way things are'. What he is looking for, by way of contrast, is a poetic language with an *estranging* rather than *familiarising* effect, a language that would radically unsettle rather than confirm and placate the expectations of a contemporary readership. 'Poetry of Departures' is, like 'Toads', a quietistic poem that manages to subdue its own rebellious instincts. At the same time, however, it might be argued that these poems create a space for different readers by inviting participation in dialogue and debate (unlike some of Larkin's heavily didactic poems in *High Windows*). In this sense they appear to be in keeping with the 'consensus' ideals of post-war society. 'Poetry of Departures' is perhaps a little more exploratory and less prescriptive than Graham Holderness suggests. In attempting to accommodate both conformist and non-conformist positions, the poem has to move beyond cliché and resort to the language of paradox. Rather than denying either of the poem's alternative impulses, the paradoxical phrasing of 'a life reprehensibly perfect' holds them in careful abeyance and shows the speaker's imagined resolution to be tentative and precarious.

In 'Poetry of Departures' the remark 'Then she undid her dress' carries the same emotional thrill for the speaker as the expression 'He walked out on the whole crowd'. The point is worth making because it provides an indication that the sexual politics of Larkin's poetry are clearly aligned with the ideas of freedom discussed here. Sex promises release and fulfilment, but for Larkin's speakers such a promise is deceptive and illusory. Except in the case of 'Wedding-Wind', these speakers are all male, and their common perception of sexual relationships involves a relinquishing of identity and power, a deep-seated fear about the loss of personal freedom. The speaker of 'Places, Loved Ones' confesses, with a mixture of disappointment and relief, that he has never 'met that special one / Who has an instant claim / On everything I own / Down to my name' (p.99). Similarly, the speaker of 'If, My Darling' insists upon his own realistic assessment of life's shortcomings and sedulously avoids any idealisation of womanhood: 'And to hear how the past is past and the future neuter / Might knock my darling off her unpriceable pivot' (p.41). What has previously been identified as political neutrality or quietism clearly extends into the realm of personal and sexual relationships. It manifests itself in terms of an intense wariness of commitment and an attempted preservation of male autonomy.

Not surprisingly, Larkin's 'love' poems are often disappointed reflections on failure, impotence and powerlessness. 'Waiting for breakfast', written in 1947 and added to a reissue of *The North Ship* in 1966, is usually seen as marking a significant transition from the influence of Yeats to that of Hardy. More importantly, though, it shows Larkin's work emerging from 'the grip of light' and seeking a surer sense of direction after the uncertainties and insecurities of the war years. What is most striking about the poem is that sexual fulfilment and artistic vocation are presented as stark alternatives. Despite a dismal and unpromising setting that is 'empty', 'wet' and 'featureless', the poem moves towards one of the most affirmative moments in Larkin's work: 'Turning, I kissed her, / Easily for sheer joy tipping the balance to love' (p.20). Just as dramatically, though, the poem then proceeds to question its own 'tender visiting', implying that such emotional excitement cannot be sustained, since it arises unexpectedly out of moments of loss and separation. There is a further suggestion that the inspiration afforded by this 'tender visiting' can be directed towards love or poetry but not both. The muse and the lover cannot exist together:

> Will you refuse to come till I have sent
> Her terribly away, importantly live
> Part invalid, part baby, and part saint?

In a characteristic moment of post-war *angst*, the speaker of 'Waiting for breakfast' declares his own diminished sense of existence and his search for some lost authenticity of being, some 'lost world' of imaginary fullness. The portentous adverbs, 'terribly' and 'importantly', suggest a degree of self-dramatisation and self-criticism, but the poem nevertheless imparts a serious and complex belief that artistic creativity necessitates an impaired and incomplete way of life. The undercurrent of religious vocabulary – 'absolvingly', 'grace' and 'saint' – points to an abstemious and almost monastic conception of the artistic life that persists throughout Larkin's poetry. As Derek Walcott has suggested, the word 'benedict' seems better than 'batchelor' as a way of describing Larkin's solitary endeavour (Walcott, 1989, p.37).

Perhaps the best example of this tension between art and sex is 'Reasons for Attendance', in which the speaker watches a group of dancers 'all under twenty-five', and reflects upon his exclusion from a scene of imagined happiness. As with 'Waiting for breakfast', looking through 'the lighted glass' is an appropriate image for trying to verify what is right or true. 'Reasons for Attendance' is a curious title, sounding much too dutiful for the occasion, but its significance becomes clear in the speaker's attempt to rationalise his own position in relation to the young dancers, while 'Attendance' carries the secondary meaning of 'attention' and so registers the speaker's determination not to be deceived. The immediate response is sensuous and physical, as in 'the wonderful feel of girls', but in characteristic fashion the poem proceeds to question and unravel its own assumptions: 'Why be out here? / But then, why be in there? / Sex, yes, but what / Is sex?' (p.80). The shared communal activity of 'couples' is weighed against the isolated artistic endeavour of the 'individual' and the poem declares its apparent preference for the special privileges of solitariness. The syntactical structure of the poem, however, implies that the decision is very far from clear cut. There is a special pleading in the rhetorical ploys and conditional utterances of the speaker – 'Or so I fancy' . . . 'Surely' . . . 'as far as I'm concerned' . . . 'if you like' – all of which culminate in the unsettling provisionality of the final lines: 'and both are satisfied, / If no one has misjudged himself. Or lied'.

As with 'Toads', we need to relate the textual structure of the poem to a post-war social structure in which attitudes to work, leisure and sexual relationships were undergoing rapid transformation. The poem intervenes in that debate about values and beliefs and, like 'Toads', insists upon the virtues of careful judgement and scrupulous honesty. Alan Sinfield offers an interesting reading of the poem by approaching it in terms of two different attitudes (the highbrow and the popular) to the same jazz subculture of the 1950s. He argues convincingly that the 'lifted, rough-tongued bell' of Art is the jazz trumpet whose 'loud and authoritative voice' is heard in stanza one (Sinfield, 1989, pp.165–6). This imagery suggests that the trumpet is also a secular version of the church bell and that the poet's calling is a kind of religious vocation, being self-denying and self-sacrificing. Jazz is certainly an important aspect of the poem's cultural context, but the social implications of the work are wide ranging. In the broadest sense, 'Reasons for Attendance' is concerned with changing codes of value and belief in a modern democratic society, a point reinforced by the prominent parallel structure of 'I . . . Believing this' and 'they . . . Believing that'. The poem achieves a fragile consensus of opinion, recognising social and cultural differences and tentatively balancing the satisfaction of the individual against that of the crowd. It is in keeping with the narrowly conceived idea of freedom in this collection of poems that happiness should be equated with the individual's decision to 'stay outside'.

The same self-denying, self-preserving impulse is evident in 'No Road', where 'fulfilment' and 'ailment' exist as uneasy half-rhymes, and where freedom is defined in terms of a willed separation between two lovers: 'To watch that world come up like a cold sun, / Rewarding others, is my liberty' (p.47). This chastened and severely circumscribed sense of freedom informs a series of poems on the relative merits of solitude and society, all of which were written in 1951 and not published until the release of Larkin's *Collected Poems* in 1988. As Blake Morrison pointed out in his review of the *Collected Poems*, these early pieces 'suggest how far an obsessive guilt and fear governed Larkin's attitude to sex, and how, for all the comfortable and confident and often very funny positions he was able eventually to take up, he remained tormented by sex, seeing it as something enclosing and destructive and hostile to artistic ambition' (Morrison, 1988, p.1152). 'Best Society', a precursor of 'Vers de Société', is a meditation on 'uncontradicting solitude' which insists upon the obvious fact that 'To love you must have someone else' (p.56). 'Marriages' cynically declares that in many cases marriage is a matter of settling for an 'undesirable' partner in whose company 'words such as liberty, / Impulse, or beauty / Shall be unmentionable' (p.63). The imaginary address 'To My Wife' is unflattering and acerbic: 'Choice of you shuts up that peacock-fan / The future was...' (p.54). To marry is to forfeit freedom and to give a permanent shape to 'boredom' and 'failure'.

Desire, then, proves to be a problematic issue in Larkin's poetry. Love promises 'to solve, and satisfy, / And set [our lives] unchangeably in order' (p.113), but it also threatens the autonomy of the self. There are deeper fears in which sexual desire seems to precipitate chaos and disorder. 'Whatever Happened', for instance, appears to be based on a turbulent sexual fantasy and invites a Freudian analysis (p.74). Sexual desire is also the subject of 'Dry-Point', as its original placing in 'Two Portraits of Sex' makes clear:

> Endlessly, time-honoured irritant,
> A bubble is restively forming at your tip.
> Burst it as fast as we can –
> It will grow again, until we begin dying.

(p.36)

The physical experience of the poem. is presented as 'a struggle' accompanied by fear and panic. The aftermath is one of disappointment and disillusionment: 'What ashen hills! what salted, shrunken lakes!'. The vocabulary of the poem consists largely of sexual puns and yet the overall treatment of the subject remains curiously oblique. The idea of representing sex in two 'portraits' is, itself, a strategy of indirection, with the punning title 'Dry-Point' referring, somewhat obscurely, to a form of copperplate engraving. Recent commentators have accounted for Larkin's unusual rendering of the subject by classifying 'Dry-Point' as a symbolist poem with a style reminiscent of nineteenth-century French poetry. However bizarre its imagery might appear, though, the poem belongs firmly to the 1950s and the prevailing discourse of sexuality in the post-war years. Its veiled allusion to Birmingham as one of the centres of the jewellery trade is a very local and immediate reference. In its suggestive and titillating imagery, the poem partakes of the emerging libertarian attitude to sex, but it also draws on the conservative reaction to that attitude by presenting sexual desire as a power to be controlled and checked. The poem recognises both the libertarian and the authoritarian views of sexual desire, seeing it both as a repressed human energy and as a potentially disintegrative and transgressive force: 'Bestial, intent, real'. Freedom from desire is pictured in terms of a remote and unattainable transcendence: 'that bare and sunscrubbed room . . . that padlocked cube of light'. These are places where, it is falsely hoped, desire can 'obtain no right of entry'. There is something peculiarly forthright about that final phrase, 'obtain no right of entry'; it belongs not to the idiom of symbolist poetry but to the social and public sphere of legislation. Its appearance at the end of the poem should remind us that even the most seemingly private and intimate poems have a wider public context. 'Dry-Point' shares the concern of 'Wires' and other poems with the boundaries and limitations of individual activity which were being steadily redrawn in the post-war era. The poem's treatment of sex is bold and experimental, but its conclusion wearily implies that this is one more area where 'freedom' proves to be illusory.

As Steve Clark has argued, the sexual politics of Larkin's verse might well be regarded as a matter of 'principled and unillusioned abstention' (Clark, 1988, p.239). Clark's essay is one of the few pieces of Larkin criticism to draw extensively on the insights of feminism and psychoanalysis, and it offers a revealing account of the suppressed eroticism and misogynist tendencies in Larkin's work. At the same time, Clark insists that there is a positive dimension to Larkin's preservation of male autonomy, and he writes favourably of 'the regenerative aspects of this refusal of illusion, this opting out of the coercive force of contemporary sexual ideology' (Clark, 1988, p.269). What Clark values is Larkin's powerful demystification of sex. The poems deny many of the myths associated with sex and in so doing reveal the extent to which such attitudes and assumptions are socially conditioned and constructed. In turn, that realisation provides an opportunity for readers to challenge prevailing sexual stereotypes. We cannot, then, discuss 'love' and 'sex' as if they were simply 'themes' of the poems, since these words operate within a specific area of social meanings and values. As readers we need to appreciate that attitudes to sexual ethics can shift dramatically within a single decade.

'Lines on a Young Lady's Photograph Album' provides a good opportunity for discussing the sexual politics of the poetry in relation to the social and cultural context of the 1950s. Its attitudes might strike some readers now as rather old-fashioned and the poem's genre might seem reminiscent of polite eighteenth-century verse. The title seems innocuous enough, and yet the 'album' becomes the occasion for a series of erotic fantasies about the woman's body, especially when 'yielded up' and 'once open' (p.71). The nature of the speaker's desire is evident in the strongly physical suggestions of 'choke' and 'hungers'. Like 'Dry-Point', 'Lines on a Young Lady's Photograph Album' belongs to a particular discourse of sexuality in which an emerging libertarian attitude is balanced against traditional ideas of sexual courtship and conduct. By 1974 this oblique eroticism had given way to the expletives of *High Windows*.

The technique of looking at 'a real girl' in a series of photographs suggests that there are further psychological and cultural dimensions to the poem. The woman is presented under the male gaze of the speaker's 'swivel eye' in a series of familiar poses – childlike, with animals or flowers, or in literary stereotypes such as Tennyson's 'sweet girl-graduate'. Any departure from these established 'norms' upsets the speaker's sense of 'proper' relationships, as we see in his equivocation over the transvestite suggestion of the woman in a trilby hat: '(Faintly disturbing, that, in several ways) – / From every side you strike at my control'. It is clear, too, that this fear of departure from convention, this preservation of the status quo, has significant class dimensions. The speaker's response to 'these disquieting chaps who loll / At ease about your earlier days' is precise and telling. Once again, the colloquial ease of Larkin's verse allows us to identify its sociolinguistic context, and in this instance we cannot fail to hear the restrained but confidently superior tones of middle-class English: 'Not quite your class, I'd say, dear, on the whole'. Photography is acknowledged as an art that is 'In every sense empirically true', but the speaker's attitudes to the photographs do not maintain the same degree of impartiality. There is a very noticeable cultural bias in the speaker's recollection of the past and his undisguised preference for 'misty parks and motors' over such 'blemishes' as 'washing-lines' and 'Hall's-Distemper boards' (a reference to a popular commercial whitewash widely used in the 1950s). The woman in the poem is not just an object of male desire but an emblem of an irrecoverable national past; she embodies all those things that 'lacerate / Simply by being over', and 'contracts' the speaker's heart 'by looking out of date'. Like many poems in *The Less Deceived*, 'Lines on a Young Lady's Photograph Album' shows a resigned and quietistic acceptance of the present, along with a corresponding sense of regret for what has passed. This is a poem in which freedom is being 'free to cry': to mourn the passing years 'without a chance of consequence'. The closing lines are invested with a lyrical and elegiac beauty that elevates 'the young lady' of the poem to the status of a mythical figure presiding over a lost paradise:

> In short, a past that no one now can share,
> No matter whose your future; calm and dry,
> It holds you like a heaven, and you lie
> Unvariably lovely there,
> Smaller and clearer as the years go by.

There is a powerful sense of loss and diminishment in the poem, made all the more painful because 'perspective brings significance'. At the same time, an apparently careless disregard for the future effectively relieves the speaker of any obligation or commitment, while a past that is 'calm and dry' leaves him 'free' of complicating relationships and actions. A similar set of emotions is at work in 'Maiden Name', where marriage is equated, in persistently negative terms, with loss of beauty. Again, the poem reveals a sceptical evasion of commitment and action; it strongly asserts its preference for what is 'past and gone', unashamedly idealising the younger woman whose 'old name shelters our faithfulness' (p.101).

The circumspect nature of *The Less Deceived* has led some critics to lose patience with Larkin's early work. Tony Pinkney, in a trenchant and forthright assessment of Larkin's place in English Studies, finds little more than futility and sterility:

> If freedom is defined as the other of sex, family, social relations, commitment, tradition or custom . . . then it is hard to see what content it might have: in effect, it vanishes into an empty formalism. All that can be said of it is that it is not this, not that: detachment tips over into nihilism, while tonally the poetry modulates into a tragic defeatism. (Pinkney, 1986, p.40)

There is, throughout the early work, a stubborn reluctance or failure to translate the idea of personal liberty into political action. Freedom is construed in narrowly existential rather than cultural terms. At the same time, however, we need to understand this reluctance not as some personal shortcoming but as a general response to post-war social change. In Shelagh Delaney's *A Taste of Honey* (1956) what looks like working-class stoicism might also be construed as a cynical and passive acceptance of the way things are: 'We don't ask for life, we have it thrust upon us' (Delaney, 1987, p.71). Although political quietism was typically the response of a disenchanted or complacent middle class, its effects were widespread in the 1950s.

The cultural value of Larkin's early poetry is that it engages in a variety of poetic forms with the beliefs and attitudes that accompanied a new and different social formation after the upheaval of the Second World War. There is a complex and distinctive relationship between the linguistic structure of the poems and the changing social structure of the post-war years, and this is clearly evident in the extent to which the poems modify traditional lyric forms by incorporating the vocabulary and phrasing of contemporary English speech. The interest and appeal of the poetry for many readers is a consequence of its significant and decisive revamping of English poetic diction. As Douglas Dunn has claimed, 'From his work in *The Less Deceived* onwards, what Larkin was involving himself with . . . was an effort to return poetry to its social lucidity on one hand, a deserved mystery and lyricism on another' (Dunn, 1987, p.4). Through its rhetorical ploys and tonal shifts, the poetry maintains a sceptical and vigilant response to the changing social order. That response often appears negative and defeatist, but the unresolved questions about selfhood and individual freedom lead finally to a new awareness of the meaning and value of human solidarity. There is, throughout *The Less Deceived*, a cautious distance between 'I' and 'We', but this notion of self-sufficient individualism cannot be sustained indefinitely. It is the search for integration and for a shared sense of communal endeavour that gives the later poems in *The Whitsun Weddings* and *High Windows* their increasing dramatic interest.

From Austerity to Affluence: *The Whitsun Weddings*

In the ten-year interval between *The Less Deceived* (1955) and *The Whitsun Weddings* (1964), the social and economic circumstances of post-war Britain had altered significantly. By the mid 1950s, the rationing of most major foodstuffs had ended, new employment opportunities were created, export targets were achieved and credit was available for the purchase of 'consumer durables': refrigerators, washing machines and television sets. By 1961 commercial television had reached the homes of eighty per cent of the population. Advertising became, in itself, a major new growth industry. A massive building programme was set up in response to new demands for housing and 'a home of one's own' became a realistic aspiration for many people. Some areas remained untouched by the economic boom, but the country was generally seen to be emerging from austerity. 1957 is often thought to be the first year of the new affluence; it was in this year that Harold Macmillan told the people of Britain that they had 'never had it so good', a phrase that was much in evidence in his election campaign two years later. *The Affluent Society* was the title of a book by Professor J.K. Galbraith, first published in 1958, and in keeping with Galbraith's thesis the term came to be associated with the uncaring materialism of the United States and with fears of a similar society being created in Britain.

The Whitsun Weddings registers the changing social and cultural climate of the late 1950s and early 1960s in an extraordinary way. The impact of mass consumerism is immediately evident in the vivid catalogue of 'desires' attracting 'residents from raw estates' in 'Here', the opening poem of the collection: 'Cheap suits, red kitchenware, sharp shoes, iced lollies, / Electric mixers, toasters, washers, driers –' (p.136). It is evident, too, in 'Mr Bleaney', with its faint disapproval of 'the jabbering set he egged her on to buy' (p.102), and in 'Afternoons', with its 'new recreation ground' and its memorable evocation of 'husbands in skilled trades', 'An estateful of washing', and 'the albums, lettered / *Our Wedding*, lying / Near the television' (p.121). The dubious glamours of advertising inform 'The Large Cool Store', 'Sunny Prestatyn' and 'Essential Beauty'. In all of these poems there is a vivid rendering of the changing social texture and a sustained interest in the changing values of its citizens. This open confrontation with the new landscape and with the lives of those who live there marks an important stage of development in Larkin's work. At the same time, it would be unwise to assess *The Whitsun Weddings* in terms of its seemingly 'accurate' social transcription, for the poems are not simply a 'reflection' of society, but a selective reordering or re-presentation of its surfaces. What the poems convey is a particular 'version' of events, a particular way of seeing and responding to the world. Significantly, there are moments in the poetry when an attempt to present a complete and unified picture of 'society' is revealed as an impossible task beyond the capacity of language.

Rather than giving us a complete and unmediated account of the England through which Larkin travels, *The Whitsun Weddings* adopts a variety of voices and perspectives through which it attempts to articulate the values and meanings of contemporary society. The attitudes implicit in the poems range from cynical outrage to plangent melancholy, while the language and syntax modulate with increasing tension between the colloquial and the lyrical. The infusion of irony and parody as distancing devices means that some poems, such as 'Naturally the Foundation will Bear Your Expenses', operate obliquely in their attitudes and responses to contemporary society. Several poems take the form of imagined dialogue ('Mr Bleaney', 'Dockery and Son', 'Reference Back'), while others create an immediate and dramatic impression of colloquial speech: 'That Whitsun I was late getting away . . .' or 'About twenty years ago / Two girls came in where I worked'. The perspective is often that of the distanced, intellectual observer, carefully reserving judgement, though proving to be fallible and sometimes mistaken in his outlook. Even so, the poems embody a range of attitudes and perspectives, and what proves to be most interesting is the dynamic and complex relationship between textual structure and social structure. In a very overt way, the poetry of *The Whitsun Weddings* functions as social discourse; its language is scored through with the conflicts and tensions of that historical turning from austerity to affluence.

Several poems in *The Whitsun Weddings* show the new consumerism to be at odds with the communal ideals of the Welfare State. These are poems which, in a spirit of political liberalism, acknowledge the potential transformation of people's lives through the acquisition of material goods and yet retain a tacit disapproval of the ugly and squalid consequences of rampant consumerism. As John Goodby suggests, 'Larkin is the uneasy, unwilling celebrator of relative affluence . . . a slightly awkward guest at the banquet of the new materialism' (Goodby, 1989, p.131). In their engagement with contemporary social ideals, the poems test the limits of 'consensus', cutting across class boundaries and enquiring into the conditions of social harmony. At the opposite poles of this enquiry are alienation and integration, and both are evident in *The Whitsun Weddings*. The symptoms of alienation are to be seen not just in the palpable violence of Titch Thomas but in the intellectual speaker's reflections on the 'quality' of life and how it might be measured. The motivating impulse behind many of the poems in *The Whitsun Weddings* ('Here', 'Mr Bleaney', 'Dockery and Son') is the search for an unalienated existence. What lies beneath these poems is a dilemma about the role of the writer / intellectual and about the value of the imagination in a changing post-war society.

The direction of 'Here' is towards a place of imaginative freedom. The absence of any obvious subject or personal pronoun in the opening stanza gives the poem a curiously disembodied effect. The main verb 'gathers' is delayed until the beginning of stanza two, and what precedes it is the experience of 'swerving': 'Swerving east ... swerving through fields ... swerving to solitude' (p.136). The poem appears to be working in a straightforwardly mimetic and descriptive way, with the prominent, repeated conjunctions of lines two, four and seven creating an effect of random accumulation. At the same time, however, there is evidence of design in the poem's selection and arrangement of its images of England, and this structuring conveys a particular set of attitudes to the contemporary landscape. The poem moves from night to day (towards the rising sun) and from the industrial heartlands and motorways to 'fields' and 'meadows'. 'Rich industrial shadows' implies that industrial sites are both abundant and a source of prosperity, while 'shadows' seems to function both literally and metaphorically. There is a sense in which industry overshadows the landscape, but there is also a lingering suggestion of England's industrial heritage. The structural dimensions of 'Here' are both spatial and temporal, both geographical and historical. We can see, for instance, how the poem confronts the modern, post-war landscape but also asserts a sense of continuity with its national past. The alliterative line 'Of skies and scarecrows, haystacks, hares and pheasants' is strongly reminiscent of an older, guidebook England. Similarly, there is something both elemental and novel, both archetypal and immediate, in Larkin's descriptions of sky and earth: 'The piled gold clouds, the shining gull-marked mud'.

The initial destination of the poem is 'a terminate and fishy-smelling / Pastoral of ships up streets'. Once again, there is an effective linking of the present and immediate place (in this case a port) with a remote and gentler sense of the national past. 'Ships up streets' is a clever use of optical illusion, reinforcing the suggestion of a town with docks, but like 'skies and scarecrows' it also has the magical quality of fable. The poem clearly draws on that species of nationalist sentiment that Raphael Samuel has identified as *urban pastoral*: a holding on to an older agricultural or seafaring image of England from within its urban and industrial present (Samuel, 1989, p.li). There is a further example of Larkin's use of urban pastoral in the image of 'Fast-shadowed wheat-fields' at the 'mortgaged half-built edges' of the new housing estates. The reference in stanza three to Wilberforce House ('the slave museum') effectively identifies the 'large town' as Hull and reaches further into its historical associations. Images of enduring civic pride ('domes', 'statues' and 'spires') are juxtaposed with those of everyday work (cranes, barges, shops). The 'stealing flat-faced trolleys' are not, as some critics have suggested, trams (which went out of service in Hull in 1945), but electrified trolley buses (which continued to operate in Hull until October 1964, three years after the poem was written). The context of the poem, then, is one in which verifiable social detail is imaginatively transposed so as to render a particular image or 'version' of a northern English landscape.

As John Lucas has pointed out, Larkin's technique in 'Here' recalls the work of Louis MacNeice, especially in its abundant compound nouns and adjectives and its tumbling catalogues of objects (Lucas, 1986). The point has been developed by Hugh Underhill, who argues that 'Louis MacNeice, in the generation preceding Larkin, is his direct forerunner as a poet of democratic urban sensibility'. There are strong likenesses between the 'desires' of 'Here' and the 'buyable beauty' of MacNeice's 'Belfast' or the assorted items behind 'the proud glass of shops' in 'Birmingham': 'Cubical scent-bottles artificial legs arctic foxes and electric mops'. The work of both poets is informed by 'an intellectual's consciousness of the mediocre and venal' (Underhill, 1989, p.189). The transferred epithet of 'A cut-price crowd' produces the kind of condescension sometimes apparent in MacNeice's work, but Larkin is perhaps less given than his predecessor to this kind of disdainful response. It is worth stressing, once again, that the most important and enduring poetic antecedents in Larkin's work belong neither to Hardy nor to Yeats, but to the poets of the 1930s, especially Auden and MacNeice. Larkin inherits an England of 'industrial shadows' and 'isolate villages', but it is an England which is now 'emptied of the urgent stresses and obligations of the thirties and the war' (Underhill, 1989, p.191).

The changed circumstances of post-war England and the absence of any clearly defined social or political direction help to explain the final movement of 'Here' towards the geographical periphery and 'the bluish neutral distance' of sea and sky. The repetition of the word 'here', the parallel phrasing and the inverted syntactical structures of the final stanza are an attempted realisation of a state of 'being' as well as a place. The prominence given to the verb 'clarifies' suggests, as in other Larkin poems, that detachment and disengagement afford a clarity of insight and perception. Rural solitude permits a different conception of 'here' from that which is afforded by the town, a mode of life apart from human progress: 'Here leaves unnoticed thicken, / Hidden weeds flower, neglected waters quicken.' 'Luminously-peopled air' refers somewhat obliquely to iridescent insects, providing a further contrast with 'the crowd' of the previous stanza. Beyond the rural loneliness and the 'shingle' beach of the coastline, however, is a destination that can never be fully known or understood: 'Here is unfenced existence: / Facing the sun, untalkative, out of reach'. These final lines of the poem carry a tremendous charge in their imaginative projection of a bright and pure element of existence beyond the quotidian perspective of the earlier stanzas. Part of the attraction of that existence, however, is that it can never be attained: unlike the 'desires' of stanza two, it is firmly 'out of reach'. The poem is able to secure a moment of repose and reflection, but its realisation of freedom is essentially a negative one, as 'unfenced' and 'untalkative' imply.

There has been a tendency in recent criticism to attribute the closing lines of 'Here' to a 'symbolist' element in Larkin's work and to acknowledge 'transcendence' as something unproblematically affirmative and positive. The weakness of such a position is that it fails to explain the desire for transcendence in relation to the social context from which it emerges. In reading 'Here' we need to understand 'transcendence' as a socially generated impulse: the response of the alienated intellectual to a changing post-war culture. 'Unfenced existence' recalls the limits and boundaries of *The Less Deceived* and reiterates the liberal conception of freedom as illusory and unattainable. In the absence of a more sustaining and realisable ideal, the poem responds to the 'desires' of the crowd in terms of complete negation, replacing instant gratification with an idea of fulfilment endlessly deferred. Given that there can be no final or permanent sense of release, the ultimate direction of the poem is not forward (since it can only gesture towards transcendence) but back, with renewed awareness of the extremes of isolation, into the communities it left behind.

David Trotter offers a further cultural explanation for what he regards as 'the obsessive patrolling of margins and thresholds in poetry since Wordsworth'. He explains that this is a tendency shown by poets 'who did not know for whom they were writing', and that it represents both a bringing into focus of the essential issues and the rediscovery of 'a generic human bond' between writer and reader (Trotter, 1984, p.6). Trotter argues that these journeys from the centre to periphery involve a release from everyday necessities and obligations, but their fundamental impulse is not so much 'separation' as 'reincorporation'. The link with Wordsworth is interesting, and the flurry of 'getting and spending' in 'Here' certainly implies a perception of a world that is 'too much with us', but there the comparison would seem to end. For all its yearning for 'elsewhere', 'Here' is a decidedly *post-romantic* poem; it seriously questions the autonomy of the imagination and the transforming powers of 'vision' on which Romantic poetic theory is posited. The limits to perception and knowledge are clearly marked in Larkin's poem. There is a sense in which the speaker's arrival at the geographical margin is also an arrival at a linguistic margin. 'Untalkative' suggests quiet, but it also implies what cannot be spoken about. Since the very language we use is 'social', to free ourselves from 'society' would necessitate freeing ourselves from language. The poem envisages a condition of wordlessness and in doing so questions its own authority as a statement about the world. The Romantic idea of the transcendent subject whose visionary power unifies the objects of perception is clearly no longer tenable.

The limits of knowledge and perception, which might be discussed more specifically in terms of Larkin's *post-romantic epistemology*, are clearly evident in the title and opening stanza of 'Ignorance':

> Strange to know nothing, never to be sure
> Of what is true or right or real,
> But forced to qualify *or so I feel*,
> Or *Well, it does seem so*:
> *Someone must know*.

(p.107)

The italicised phrases in this extract are colloquial expressions which have a common currency, and in a characteristic way the poem employs the plural pronoun 'we' to reassert its sense of a shared dilemma. This perception of common distress and common destiny makes solidarity and integration desirable and necessary; it helps to break down distinctions between self and others. Frequently, Larkin's poems move towards a generalising statement which encompasses 'all of us', and yet the poetry cannot entirely efface the deep divisions which continue to operate in post-war society. In a highly illuminating discussion of *The Whitsun Weddings*, Michael O'Neill points to the importance of 'difference' as a structuring principle in Larkin's work and concludes that 'The volume's final assertion of what is common to and best in our humanity emerges from the poet's troubled recognition of and regard for "difference"' (O'Neill, 1988, p.197). Larkin's technique is to acknowledge the diversity of opinions and lifestyles that constitutes the 'new' society, while at the same time seeking to accommodate these differences by appealing to a common set of values and meanings. It need hardly be said that such a technique is in keeping with the political aspirations of post-war social democracy and the continuing emphasis on the need for 'consensus'.

Differences of class and culture are much more pronounced in *The Whitsun Weddings* than in Larkin's earlier volumes. The restlessness and rootlessness of 'Here' arise not only from different conceptions of place but from an implicit contrast between the solitary spectator and the collective lives of those he describes: 'Workmen at dawn', 'residents from raw estates', and 'grim head-scarved wives'. Similarly, 'Mr Bleaney' dramatises cultural differences, not only between the new tenant and his predecessor but between the tenant and the landlady. One of the most impressive aspects of 'Mr Bleaney' is the way in which it utilises a variety of linguistic registers and creates a strong sense of interpersonal speech that cuts across the poem's insistent rhyming quatrains. Part of the poem's colloquial effect derives from strongly marked pauses (the use of caesura) and rapid enjambment within and between stanzas. The poem opens with the voice of the landlady, followed by the depressed observations of the prospective tenant:

> 'This was Mr Bleaney's room. He stayed
> The whole time he was at the Bodies, till

> They moved him.' Flowered curtains, thin and frayed,
> Fall to within five inches of the sill . . .'
>
> (p.102)

The only direct speech attributed to the tenant is his resigned acceptance, 'I'll take it', and yet the interaction between his thought patterns and the speech patterns of the landlady creates an impression of dialogue. At the same time, there is a noticeable tension between the landlady's implicit expectations of the new arrival ('Mr Bleaney took / My bit of garden properly in hand') and his own undisguised disappointment that there is 'no room for books or bags'. As J.R. Watson has convincingly argued, the speaker in 'Mr Bleaney' is essentially *apart* in terms of his language and behaviour: 'The socio-linguistic point is made when the landlady does *not* say "During the period of his stay here, Mr Bleaney was able to give me a considerable amount of help in the garden"' (Watson, 1989, p.150).

The obvious contrast in the poem, which many commentators overlook, is between the intellectual concerns of the speaker and the manual preoccupations of Mr Bleaney. 'The Bodies', a local term for a car body plant, especially in the Midlands, effectively identifies Bleaney as a car worker. Differences of class and culture are evident in the very manner with which the speaker proceeds to analyse the lifestyle of Mr Bleaney; he cannot altogether avoid judging the other man according to the meagre surroundings he inhabited (it is frequently pointed out that 'Bleaney' is an elision of 'bleak' and 'mean' and therefore invites such a judgement). Although Bleaney appears to have persuaded the landlady to buy a television set, the place is uncomfortably austere: 'Bed, upright chair, sixty-watt bulb'. The speaker establishes a superficial relationship with Mr Bleaney through the colloquial idiom of 'stub my fags / On the same saucer-souvenir' and also appears to understand why 'He kept on plugging at the four aways'. Bleaney's insistence on 'doing the pools' hints at desires beyond the unglamorous holiday with 'the Frinton folk' and 'Christmas at his sister's house in Stoke'.

It is clear, however, that a significant shift of perspective occurs in the speaker's mind between the assured statement 'I know his habits' and the poem's disarming final admission: 'I don't know'. The point of transition is signalled by the decisive halt of stanza five and the opening conjunction of stanza six:

But if he stood and watched the frigid wind
Tousling the clouds, lay on the fusty bed
Telling himself that this was home, and grinned,
And shivered, without shaking off the dread

That how we live measures our own nature,
And at his age having no more to show
Than one hired box should make him pretty sure
He warranted no better, I don't know.

The convoluted syntax of these closing stanzas seems to initiate a more imaginative and sympathetic engagement with the life of Mr Bleaney than the speaker has previously shown. The emphasis here is on what Bleaney might have thought and felt, and not simply on his possessions and habits, and yet the speaker retains an appalled fascination with what Mr Bleaney 'had to show'. This anxiety about 'what one is' in relation to 'what one has' might seem overstated to later generations of readers, but it is certainly not unusual in the context of post-war social and cultural change. 'Mr Bleaney' was written in 1955 at that very point where 'austerity' was about to give way to 'affluence'. The anxiety within the poem is generated by the uncertain role of the writer/intellectual in that changing social context. Like several poems in *The Whitsun Weddings*, 'Mr Bleaney' is an attempt to understand the self in relation to the values and beliefs of others. The 'hired box' and the equally ambiguous expression 'till / They moved him' suggest that Mr Bleaney has already passed on and serve to remind us of a common destiny that 'we' all share. The poem's search for common ground or consensus does not, however, cancel out its preoccupation with social differences.

Most commentators have argued that the poem concludes with an unexpected identification between the speaker and Mr Bleaney. The closing statement, 'I don't know', can be seen as a refusal to pass easy judgement on Bleaney, but it also effectively marks the limits of the speaker's enquiry. There is, in addition, a stiffly intellectual and curiously formal response in the phrase 'warranted no better' (not 'deserved' but 'warranted'), which tactfully avoids the reasons for Mr Bleaney's discomfort. The all-pervading sense of 'not knowing' conveyed in 'Ignorance' extends in this instance into the area of class and cultural relations. 'Differences' are subsumed by this condition of ignorance and are treated as merely incidental or accidental. In both 'Mr Bleaney' and 'The Whitsun Weddings', the speaker's encounter with the experiences of others, of a different social class, is presented as chance: 'So it *happens* that I lie / Where Mr Bleaney lay' (italics added). 'Mr Bleaney' is a valuable and revealing poem in the way it dramatises differences in social and cultural outlook, but the subtlety of its technique is in evading rather than exploring those differences.

The withering domestic sadness of 'Mr Bleaney' pervades a number of poems in *The Whitsun Weddings*. In all of these poems there is a strong attraction to the particularity of objects and possessions: the woman's gloves and shoes in 'Broadcast', or the music covers which have been 'kept' for years in 'Love Songs in Age': 'One bleached from lying in a sunny place, / One marked in circles by a vase of water, / One mended . . .' (p.140). Usually these personal items are an indication of a certain way of life, or of certain expectations and desires. In 'Home is so Sad' we are asked to view a deserted room and imagine 'how it was': 'Look at the pictures and the cutlery. / The music in the piano stool. That vase' (p.119). These things are a measure of how we live and what we have, and yet they cannot prevent or withold a yearning for a deeper sense of fulfilment and achievement. The widow in 'Love Songs in Age' finds her songs while 'looking for something else' (the noun is suitably and characteristically vague), and what the songs project is an ideal of love: 'Still promising to solve and satisfy, / And set unchangeably in order' (p.113). A desire for pattern and order in life, whether in the shape of objects or ideals, is constantly frustrated by what is unplanned and unforeseen. In Larkin's estimation, our aspirations to something better are always defeated: 'A joyous shot at how things ought to be, / Long fallen wide' (p.119).

'Nothing To Be Said' resorts to a blatantly amateurish anthropology in its claim that life for all classes and cultures is ultimately the same since it is subject to inevitable extinction. From this perspective, the lives of 'cobble-close families / In mill-towns on dark mornings' are really no different from those of 'nomads among stones' or 'small-statured cross-faced tribes' (p.138). Once again, there is a sustained interest in the question of 'how we live' and a conviction that all human activity – work, play and prayer – is eclipsed by the shadow of death. What might be regarded as 'separate' ways of 'building, benediction, / Measuring love and money' are all 'Ways of slow dying'. Whether it is treated with disregard or dread, the stubborn fact of death seems to cancel out any thoughts of a better life: 'And saying so to some / Means nothing; others it leaves / Nothing to be said'. As with 'Mr Bleaney', an appeal to the limits of language and perception, an expression of bafflement in the face of the unknown, effectively rules out any further consideration of how best to structure and organise 'life'.

In 'Self's the Man' a comparison between two lifestyles seems to reveal essential differences but in the end proves very little. From the outset, the speaker's blustery expostulation leads us to question his assumptions:

> Oh, no one can deny
> That Arnold is less selfish than I.
> He married a woman to stop her getting away
> Now she's there all day,
>
> And the money he gets for wasting his life on work
> She takes as her perk
> To pay for the kiddies' clobber and the drier
> And the electric fire . . .
>
> (p.117)

The doggerel-like metre, with its banal rhymes and familiar, colloquial idiom, declares the speaker's disenchantment with family life and household goods. The negative, exaggerated motives which the speaker attributes to Arnold appear to weigh the arguments for solitude heavily in his own favour. As with 'Mr Bleaney', however, the speaker reverses his initial judgements and concedes that 'he and I are the same'. The final stanza allows for a further qualification in which the limits of 'knowledge' are once again decisive:

> Only I'm a better hand
> At knowing what I can stand
> Without them sending a van –
> Or I suppose I can.
>
> (p.118)

The closing note of vulnerability and the casual but fearful suggestion of breakdown in 'sending the van' upset and undermine the speaker's declared autonomy and put in doubt the secure male 'self' of the title. The language of the poem works effectively to portray Arnold's different, working-class existence in such expressions as 'a read at the evening paper' and 'the nippers to wheel round the houses'. Characteristically, though, the poem imposes severe limits on the extent to which such lifestyles can be transformed. The technique is always to deflect such considerations into the realm of the unknown and the insoluble. In 'Days', an over-confident and childishly simplistic assertion of what we do with time shifts into a more sombre reflection with the insistent question: 'Where can we live but days?' (p.67). The poem concludes that posing such existential questions intrudes upon the concerns of those who are ultimately responsible for our spiritual and physical well-being and 'Brings the priest and the doctor / In their long coats / Running over the fields'. Far better, then, to sit still and be quiet.

'Dockery and Son' is a further reflection on alternative ways of living, with 'paternity' being a critical issue. The poem opens with the speaker's jocular account of a visit to his old college, but the suggestion (in the phrase 'Death-suited') that the occasion is a funeral allows the poem to develop into a more sombre reflection on the passing of time. The close proximity of the verbs 'Locked' and 'ignored' reifies the speaker's sense of exclusion from where he 'used to live', while the view of Oxford from a train window provides a suitably diminished perspective: 'Canal and clouds and colleges subside / Slowly from view' (p.152). A very different England is evident in the speaker's recollection of 'the fumes and furnace-glares of Sheffield, where I changed, / And ate an awful pie'. The verb 'changed' carries suggestions not just of swapping trains but of changing to another way of life. That 'awful pie' is unexpectedly juxtaposed with a moment of lyrical beauty in which the speaker contrasts his own uncertain direction with the constancy of the 'strong / Unhindered moon'. Once again, the occasion provides the speaker with an opportunity for 'measuring existence': in this case, for 'finding out how much had gone from life'. As with 'Mr Bleaney', the vocabulary of the poem is strongly implicated in the imperatives of post-war affluence and acquisitiveness, of wanting and having: 'To have no son, no wife, / No house or land still seemed quite natural' (there is no distinction here between relatives and possessions). Dockery, we are told, 'must have taken stock / Of what he wanted'. The determining influence of a society increasingly swayed by fashion and personal possessions is clearly evident in the poem's account of how 'assumptions' come to dominate existence: 'They're more a style / Our lives bring with them: habit for a while, / Suddenly they harden into all we've got / And how we got it'. The point is underlined by the apparent contrast between the biblical 'got' and the crudely acquisitive 'got'. The question 'Where do these / Innate assumptions come from?' vanishes into the strangely imprecise image of blinding 'sand-clouds', leaving an all-enveloping nothing: 'For Dockery a son, for me nothing / Nothing with all a son's harsh patronage'. A familir technique in Larkin's poems is to minimise social differences in the face of certain extinction, thereby giving authority to an all-inclusive statement:

> Life is first boredom, then fear.
> Whether or not we use it, it goes,
> And leaves what something hidden from us chose,
> And age, and then the only end of age.
>
> (p.153)

In this instance the statement about common destiny seems unjust-ified and out of all proportion to the experience that has prompted it. Some readers will resist the presumed 'we' of the final stanza or object to the poem's refusal to clarify that hidden 'something'. What makes 'Dockery and Son' such an imposing piece of writing, however, is that its bleak and uncompromising sentiments appeal for recognition and common agreement while simultaneously pro-voking dissent.

'Something', like 'nothing', is one of those words that allow Larkin's poems to remain uncommitted about what determines the nature of 'being', while retaining a sense of urgency and distress in response to common suffering. The young couples in 'Afternoons' find that 'Something is pushing them / To the side of their own lives' (p.121), and in 'Ambulances' the experience of being 'carried in and stowed' is followed by 'the sudden shut of loss / Round something nearly at an end' (p.132). The word 'all' occurs with similar frequency in Larkin's lexicon, usually as a way of reinforcing what appear to be common dilemmas and disappointments. 'Faith Heal-ing' complains that 'all's wrong', and registers its disbelief in the practices of an American evangelist with the concluding phrase: 'and all time has disproved' (p.126). What gives 'Ambulances' its impressive authority is its relentless insistence that 'All streets in time are visited' and its closing assertion that to be transported by ambulance 'Brings closer what is left to come, / And dulls to distance all we are'. The poem is able to arrive at that all-encompassing realisation only by concentrating simultaneously on the particularity of the lives in question:

> Then children strewn on steps or road,
> Or women coming from the shops
> Past smells of different dinners, see
> A wild white face that overtops
> Red stretcher-blankets momently
> As it is carried in and stowed,
>
> And sense the solving emptiness
> That lies just under all we do,
> And for a second get it whole,
> So permanent and blank and true.

Like 'the awful pie' in 'Dockery and Son', 'smells of different dinners' leads unexpectedly to a moment of heightened intensity, while its seemingly mundane quality reinforces the sense of common destiny that follows. 'Solving emptiness' functions enigmatically and ambiguously since it is able to inflect a sense of both 'resolving' and 'dissolving'. The poem seems to speak with 'timeless' and 'universal' wisdom, and yet its ideas are those of a very distinctive agnostic consciousness. Larkin's espousal of late twentieth-century agnosticism is evident not just in the poem's residual religious vocabulary ('Closed like confessionals' or '*Poor soul*, they whisper . . .') but also in the conviction that individual lives are both 'random' and 'unique'. What gives that individual life a claim upon the reader's attention is 'what cohered in it across / The years'. In the absence of a more sustaining and unifying belief, Larkin's speakers resort to the secular principle of coherence. This notion of 'coherence', however, is not only a pseudo-religious principle; it is also an idea that is central to English political liberalism and to the underlying aspirations of post-war consensus. It is this search for coherence that gives scope and momentum to what many commentators regard as Larkin's finest poem: 'The Whitsun Weddings'.

The genesis of 'The Whitsun Weddings' was a railway journey which Larkin made in July 1955. Drafts of the poem were prepared in the summer of 1957, but it was not completed until October 1958.

Like 'Here', 'The Whitsun Weddings' offers a sweeping, panoramic view of the contemporary landscape and uses the journey as a way of structuring its multiple and disparate perceptions. The breadth and energy of the poem derive in part from its search for coherence and unity, not only among the changing landscapes of post-war England but among the lives of those who dwell there. The landscapes of 'The Whitsun Weddings' range over town and country, over places of work and leisure, and the novelty of the poem's presentation lies in its patterning of seemingly random observations and occurrences: the insertion of 'a cooling tower', for instance, between an Odeon cinema and a cricket pitch. Larkin's England is a place of long established agricultural and industrial labour: 'Wide farms went by, short-shadowed cattle, and / Canals with floatings of industrial froth . . .' (p.114). It is also, however, a place that reveals the distinctive signs of post-war reconstruction, as we see in the speaker's disapproving response to 'the next town, new and nondescript'.

The poem makes extensive use of the urban pastoral perspective adopted in 'Here' to impose a sense of unity and continuity upon geographical and historical divisions. Sometimes this takes the form of metaphoric substitution ('acres of dismantled cars') and some-times direct simile ('Its postal districts packed like squares of wheat'), but the rapid movement of the train is, in itself, a device which collapses spatial and temporal distances and creates a striking effect of simultaneity as well as change: 'Now fields were building-plots, and poplars cast / Long shadows over major roads . . .' It is important to stress that 'The Whitsun Weddings' is a poem of social and cultural attitudes and not just direct, mimetic description. As with 'Mr Bleaney', the speaker of the poem defines his role in contemporary society in terms of 'reading', and his position as 'intellectual' largely determines his presentation of events. The poem highlights differ-ences in taste and value, as we see in the speaker's comic but rather prim response to 'girls / In parodies of fashion'. The fourth stanza offers a characteristically middle-class perspective of 'common life':

> The fathers with broad belts under their suits
> And seamy foreheads; mothers loud and fat;
> An uncle shouting smut; and then the perms,
> The nylon gloves and jewellery-substitutes,
> The lemons, mauves, and olive-ochres that
>
> Marked off the girls unreally from the rest.

The details of dress and behaviour in this passage immediately signal that its perspective belongs to someone of a different class and culture, someone who is unimpressed by what he perceives as the tawdry, second-rate products of the time: the gloves are nylon, not silk, and the jewellery is a cheap imitation of the real thing. The poem accordingly leaves itself open to charges of snobbery and elitism. The point has been made most forcefully and eloquently by Stan Smith:

> This condescension, turning to resentment before the actual typicality of what is supposed to be uniquely individual life, pervades the poetry of the post-war period. It expresses the renewed anxiety of a traditional liberal individualism that has survived into an era of welfare-state social democracy, where mass tastes and values prevail, and the charming yokels of an earlier pastoral have turned into menacingly actual travelling companions, claiming equal rights with the egregious and refined spectator of their shoddy ordinariness. (Smith, 1982, p.176)

There is undoubtedly a degree of condescension in the lines quoted, which is hardly mitigated by their implicit desire for something better. At the same time, however, this condescension is attributed to a speaker whose caricaturing tendencies are the product of a limited knowledge and vision. In a revealing way, that caricaturing exposes the nature of class consciousness and shows how social differences and divisions persist in the shadow of a hopeful consensus.

The interest of 'The Whitsun Weddings' lies not just in *what* is seen but *how* it is seen, and it is the particularity and relativity of vision that is stressed: 'each face seemed to define / Just what it saw'. The speaker's perception proves to be fallible and deficient; he reveals how on a second and more curious inspection he 'saw it all again in different terms', but even then the poem sedulously avoids making any final judgement of what the day's events might signify. The interaction of personal pronouns – I, We, They – allows the poem to move repeatedly from the detached perspective of the speaker towards a more participatory, communal perspective: 'Free at last, / And loaded with the sum of all they saw, / We hurried towards London, shuffling gouts of steam'. The implications of 'Free at last' continue to echo throughout the poem as it moves into a closer engagement with the hopes and expectations of the newly-wed

couples. It is the movement of the train in relation to the sun that
determines the speaker's particular angles of vision, hence the
reference to 'blinding windscreens' and a hothouse that 'flashed
uniquely'. There is something both random and 'unique' about
individual moments of perception, as the poem suggests in its
brilliant cinematic still of 'someone running up to bowl'. But while
the sun illuminates a changing landscape, it also 'destroys / The
interest of what's happening in the shade'. The speaker explores a
variety of perspectives in attempting to reach a consensus of
understanding, a shared set of meanings, until finally the sun is
replaced by the image of rain falling somewhere 'out of sight'. The
poem contemplates the possibility of an integrated, unified vision, as
well as its ultimate dissolution.

The powerful momentum with which 'The Whitsun Weddings'
closes is generated by the tension between contingency – the idea of
the journey as 'a frail / Travelling coincidence' – and the continuing
desire for lasting significance: 'how their lives would all contain this
hour'. It is the absence of any such transcendental meaning that
shapes the final outlook of the poem, as it does in 'Here' and 'High
Windows'. Larkin's habitual method is to close that seeming gap
with a spatial metaphor – in this case 'an arrow shower' – while
leaving its location sufficiently vague ('somewhere') to allow for the
possibility of fulfilment. Larkin told one of his interviewers that he
intended 'to give an unqualified assent to hopefulness at the end of
the poem' (Haffenden, 1981, pp.124–5), and yet the suggestion of
Cupid's arrow and the more positive, fertile associations of 'rain'
cannot altogether eliminate the uneasiness and uncertainty associated with the poem's final 'sense of falling'. Several critics, including
Tom Paulin (1990) and Martin Stannard (1989), have perceived in
the arrow-shower an oblique reference to Agincourt in the famous
wartime film of *Henry V*, and therefore a rueful and ironic echo of
lost English glory. The Shakespearean source of this reference is
confirmed by Jean Hartley in *Philip Larkin, The Marvell Press and
Me* (1989).

Surprisingly, very few critics have interpreted 'The Whitsun
Weddings' in terms of the ritualistic associations of its title. David
Trotter has suggested that the poem involves 'a rite of passage',
which in most cultures accompanies a change of place or condition,
such as birth, marriage and death: 'these are agnostic journeys ...
which celebrate the connection between individual experience and

shared meaning if and when it occurs . . .' (Trotter, 1984, pp.180–2). This mythical, anthropological dimension to the poem is evident in its recognition that the weddings are moments of painful loss and separation as well as celebration. Marriage is like 'a happy funeral . . . a religious wounding'. The specific occasion of the poem, however, is Whitsun or Pentecost, as described in the Acts of the Apostles: 'And when the day of Pentecost was fully come, they were all with one accord in one place'. The New Testament tells of how the Apostles were visited by the Holy Spirit and were empowered to speak in languages not their own. Larkin's poem adheres to these ideals of unity and coherence while endowing them with a secular rather than Christian significance. In the absence of any transcendental meaning, what the poem resorts to is a belief in 'providence'. This providential ideology is a salient feature of English liberalism, as Fredric Jameson has argued in his study of E. M. Forster's *Howards End*; it manifests itself in a literature which 'transforms chance contacts, coincidence, the contingent and random encounters between isolated subjects, into a Utopian glimpse of achieved community' (Jameson, 1988, p.18). It is this glimpse of 'achieved community', however ephemeral, that gives 'The Whitsun Weddings' its stature and appeal.

The extent to which life is shaped by what is fortuitous and incidental is the subject of 'Send No Money', in which the speaker asks Time to tell the truth and is given the reply: *'Sit here, and watch the hail / Of occurrence clobber life out / To a shape no one sees* – (p.146). Later in life the speaker records that experience has predictably been determined by 'the blows of what happened to happen'. The colloquial idiom and conversational tone give the poem a broad, democratic appeal, and yet the outlook it registers is heavily deterministic and obdurately defeatist:

> What does it prove? Sod all.
> In this way I spent youth,
> Tracing the trite untransferable
> Truss-advertisement, truth.

What proves to be most interesting about the poem is the way in which its disenchantment with the unreliability of 'truth' is couched in the language of contemporary advertising. The title, 'Send No Money', cynically imitates the hoodwinking techniques of advertis-

ing with their 'genuine' appeal to the customer. The torrent of
alliteration in the final lines is contemptuous and dismissive, but it is
also worth noting that 'untransferable' belongs to the discourse of
commerce and insurance, while 'Truss-advertisement' implies that
'truth', like the suspect pseudo-medical products in newspaper
advertisements, offers only an illusory comfort and support. The
effect of such language is to reinforce the connection between the
speaker's strong sense of disillusionment and the deceptive economic
practices of modern consumerism.

'The Large Cool Store' reveals how the most intimate dreams and
desires are manipulated by the rampant consumerism of the early
1960s. This time issues of class and gender are shown to be deeply
implicated in the prevailing economic system. 'The large cool store'
with its 'cheap clothes' calls to mind 'the weekday world of those /
Who leave at dawn low terraced houses / Timed for factory, yard
and site' (p.135). The poem focuses on working-class lives as a way
of reinforcing the disparity between the grim actuality of day-to-day
life and the world of fantasy stimulated by the new shopping ethos.
In contrast to the 'heaps of shirts and trousers' are 'the stands of
Modes for Night', where 'Lemon, sapphire, moss-green, rose / Bri-
Nylon Baby-Dolls and Shorties / Flounce in clusters'. This con-
sumerist exoticism encourages a 'matching', not only of people and
clothes but of men and women. In referring to our 'young unreal
wishes', the speaker shows solidarity with 'their sort' and registers
his dissent from a system that manipulates sexual ideals and desires.
The function of that system is to disguise the crude processes of
exchange by turning 'women' into a product indistinguishable from
the clothing on sale: 'synthetic, new, / And natureless in ecstasies'.

'Essential Beauty', written a year later than 'The Large Cool
Store' in June 1962, ironically contrasts Plato's world of ideal forms
with the giant advertisement hoardings that belong to the super-
structure of the new consumer industry:

> In frames as large as rooms that face all ways
> And block the ends of streets with giant loaves,
> Screen graves with custard, cover slums with praise
> Of motor-oil and cuts of salmon, shine
> Perpetually these sharply-pictured groves
> Of how life should be.
>
> (p.144)

There is a further contrast between the scene of urban decay and the images of pastoral England which are cynically employed as a means of boosting sales. 'Groves' harks back to a much older, Arcadian and 'poetic' England, while the poem's elevated visual perspective and its coupled rhymes help to merge the reality of the street with the unreality of the projected consumer paradise: 'High above the gutter / A silver knife sinks into golden butter, / A glass of milk stands in a meadow'. The second stanza undercuts the serenity of the advertisements with forceful reminders of sickness, age and death: 'dark raftered pubs ... filled with white-clothed ones from tennis-clubs' are made to entertain 'the boy puking his heart out in the Gents'. Like 'The Large Cool Store', the poem exposes the way in which consumerism serves to construct and reinforce gender stereotypes. Cigarettes, for instance, trade on masculine desire and offer in their special brand of advertising 'that unfocused she / No match lit up, nor drag ever brought near'. The poem's closing image of the woman 'Smiling, and recognising, and going dark' signals its distance and dissent from a crudely exploitative economy.

If Larkin's poems inveigh against the coercive ideology of modern consumerism, they often seem depressingly resigned in the face of exploitation and unable to envisage·a better future. Instead, they revert to the image of a distant England, an England that lies uneasily between historical fact and patent fiction. 'MCMXIV' appears to record a specific moment in English social history, with its opening reference to 'Those long uneven lines' of men enlisting for war (p.127). The Roman numerals of the title suggest a memorial for the war dead and accordingly give a sense of fixity and finality to the year in question. The evocative details of the poem serve to emphasise differences between 'then' and 'now': there is a suggestion of a more modest and respectful society, for instance, in the reference to 'dark-clothed children at play / Called after kings and queens'. There is a strong contrast, too, between the garish advertisement hoardings in 'Essential Beauty' and the old-fashioned 'tin advertisements / For cocoa and twist'. As the poem proceeds, however, the distinction between historical detail and fictional creation is blurred, and the thought of the pubs 'open all day' initiates a rhapsodic movement:

> And the countryside not caring:
> The place-names all hazed over

> With flowering grasses, and fields
> Shadowing Domesday lines
> Under wheat's restless silence;
> The differently-dressed servants
> With tiny rooms in huge houses,
> The dust behind limousines . . .

'Domesday' asserts an idea of continuity in national history, linking pre-war England with an essential rural heritage, but it also hints obliquely at the impending catastrophe of the First World War, as does the charged pathos of 'the men / Leaving the gardens tidy'. The effect of this pastoral elegy is to make the old class hierarchy appear as natural as wheat, and yet the discrepancies in power and status unsettle the poem's declarations of 'innocence'. The repetition of 'Never such innocence' gives emotional emphasis to the poem's sense of loss and yet it inevitably raises doubts about whether such innocence *ever* existed. In this sense, the impulse behind the poem is not so much nostalgia as an awareness of the desirability and yet fallibility of national ideals. This would seem to be the substance behind Larkin's comment that 'MCMXIV' and 'Send No Money' are 'representative examples of the two kinds of poem I sometimes think I write: the beautiful and the true . . . One of the jobs of the poem is to make the beautiful seem true and the true beautiful, but in fact the disguise can usually be penetrated' (Gibson, 1973, p.102). The steady enumeration of detail in 'MCMXIV' creates an effect of impressions gathered at second hand from a sepia photograph. What lends coherence to these impressions is a persistent use of the conjunction 'and'. The poem consists of a single sentence divided into several co-ordinate clauses, with the main verb being replaced by a series of present-tense participles: 'Standing', 'Grinning', 'caring', 'flowering', 'Shadowing', 'Leaving', 'Lasting'. For all its seemingly 'realistic' detail, 'MCMXIV' is essentially an act of rhetorical persuasion.

There is in Larkin's conception of England an ideal of tradition and duty that persists alongside an increasing dismay at the ravages of consumerism. Paradoxically, it is 'the importance of elsewhere', as the poem of that title suggests, that brings to mind these civic obligations and commitments. The experience of living in Ireland is one of 'strangeness' and 'difference', and yet it is this recognition of another culture and another speech that permits and enables contact (p.104). The feeling of estrangement leads the speaker to reflect on his own culture:

> Living in England has no such excuse:
> These are my customs and establishments
> It would be much more serious to refuse.
> Here no elsewhere underwrites my existence.

The poem slips surprisingly (and perhaps too easily) into conformity and yet the speaker's sense of being 'separate' in Ireland raises questions about precisely *what* constitutes national identity and selfhood. Living 'outside' England creates an unsettling perspective in which 'existence' is seen not as some absolute state but as a structure of rules and regulations. The verb 'underwrites' suggests 'guarantees' or 'secures', but it also reveals the extent to which 'existence' is subject to legal and economic restrictions. While recognising the 'seriousness' of national unity, the poem also denies any easy or natural association between person and place.

A strong sense of civic obligation and a deeply felt commitment to the national past is evident in 'Naturally the Foundation will Bear Your Expenses'. This time, the poem takes the form of a caustic satirical attack on a particularly insidious and objectionable brand of careerism. As Derek Walcott has commented, 'There is not a more acid portrait of English academic hypocrisy' (Walcott, 1989, p.38). The title points sarcastically to a selfish squandering of financial resources, but the poem is preoccupied more generally with the abandonment of that entire tradition of liberal humanism epitomised by the work of E.M. Forster. 'Morgan Forster' is now the subject of casual name-dropping, and there is a trenchant irony in the suggestion of the speaker making his own 'passage' to India (going down 'Auster' means flying south), where a former Empire has become a playground for the academic élite. The poem resorts to mockery in its suggestion that this modern, cosmopolitan scholar has befriended Professor P. Lal, whose attempts to promote the use of 'Indian English' were often treated with derision by conservative intellectuals in the 1960s. In a slick and self-satisfied jargon, the speaker reflects upon his own academic good fortune and declares his ambition to spin out a lecture given at the University of California into a book for Chatto and Windus and a radio programme for the BBC:

> Hurrying to catch my Comet
>   One dark November day,
> Which soon would snatch me from it
>   To the sunshine of Bombay,
> I pondered pages Berkeley
>   Not three weeks since had heard,
> Perceiving Chatto darkly
>   Through the mirror of the Third.
>
> (p.134)

This first stanza contains an ironic invocation of St Paul's Epistle (1. Cor. 13. 11–12), in which seeing as a child is equated with 'seeing through a glass, darkly'. The irony is redoubled in the speaker's petulant outburst, 'O when will England grow up?'. The central stanza of the poem records the speaker's dismissive attitude to the Remembrance Day service in London and his disdainful response to the 'colourless and careworn' crowd who delay his taxi. In keeping with companion pieces in *The Whitsun Weddings*, the poem surveys 'the state of the nation' and considers its values and ideals. In its fierce contrast between self-seeking individualism and communal rites and obligations, and in its cutting satirical technique, the poem also anticipates some of the most striking developments in Larkin's final collection of poems, *High Windows*.

The End of Consensus: *High Windows*

Very few decades in British history have had such a distinctive social character as the 1960s, and the prevailing image of the time is still one of youthful rebellion and hedonistic pleasure. In some ways, however, the lively, colourful surfaces of the decade served to disguise rather than highlight its social divisions and often created a diversion from the grim economic problems of the time. In 1964, the year in which *The Whitsun Weddings* was published, a new Labour government came to power under Harold Wilson, promising to transform Britain through 'the white heat of technological revolution'. The economic difficulties it faced, though, were insurmountable and the devaluation of the pound became inevitable. The Conservative government elected in 1970 proved no more capable of handling the economy and suffered a humiliating defeat four years later, amid widespread industrial unrest. By the early 1970s the post-war consensus of political opinion which had helped to establish the benefits of the Welfare State was clearly at an end, the lines of ideological conflict and division were becoming more obvious, and the country was facing a severe economic recession. *High Windows*, published in 1974, marks the end of consensus in a profoundly unsettling and highly polemical way. Larkin's final volume of poems was to be his most provocative and disturbing collection, but also his most experimental in style and technique. There is an unmistakable correspondence between the breakdown of social consensus and the fractured linguistic contours of Larkin's final poems. If *High Windows* is sometimes savage and vehement in its outlook, it is also the most socially committed and ideologically engaged collection of poems that Larkin produced.

Between 1964 and 1967 the Labour government struggled to keep the pound stable at the value which had been fixed in 1949. In the event, it had to cut down on a wide range of spending and in 1967 took the decision to call back British troops from Aden. Early in 1968 the government announced that all British forces would leave the area 'East of Suez' by 1971. Larkin's ironic diatribe, 'Homage to a Government', acknowledges the economic crisis but interprets it simplistically in terms of idleness and greed. The poem makes its point in a repetitive and desultory idiom:

> Next year we shall be living in a country
> That brought its troops home for lack of money.
> The statues will be standing in the same
> Tree-muffled squares, and look nearly the same.
> Our children will not know it's a different country.
> All we can hope to leave them now is money.
>
> (p.171)

The poem edges towards satire but its effect is crudely polemical. A feigned innocence disguises the extent of the poem's political naïvety. As Stan Smith has argued, 'Homage to a Government' 'dissociates the whole question of decolonisation from its confused and complex history, and presents it as simply one more venal betrayal in the story of a vulgar and degrading social democracy' (Smith, 1982, p.179). A much briefer but no less acerbic piece was composed by Larkin in the same year (1969), during the 'Black Paper' discussions about educational policy:

> When the Russian tanks roll westward, what defence for you
> and me?
> Colonel Sloman's Essex Rifles? The Light Horse of L.S.E.?
>
> (p.172)

The tendency, once again, is to relate Britain's apparent military decline to a perceived lack of moral fibre and a misguided sense of direction in the late 1960s. What produces Larkin's chagrin is the suggestion that spending on education has outweighed spending on defence. The target this time is student militancy and the progressive educational policies of the London School of Economics and Essex University (under its Vice Chancellor, Albert Sloman). In the wake of Soviet peace initiatives and the relentless economic cutbacks inflicted on educational institutions after 1979, Larkin's satirical squib seems all the more reactionary and offensive.

There is further evidence of Larkin's overtly polemical style in 'Going, Going', which first appeared as part of a report commissioned by the Department of the Environment in 1972, printed over a photograph of industrial Teesside. Anticipating that England will become 'First slum of Europe', the poem modulates into a regressive pastoralism. Again, the culprit is money, with the auctioneer's cry of 'Going, Going' suggesting that the countryside is being sold off:

> And that will be England gone,
> The shadows, the meadows, the lanes,
> The guildhalls, the carved choirs.
> There'll be books; it will linger on
> In galleries; but all that remains
> For us will be concrete and tyres.
>
> (p.189)

In its concern for the environment the poem responds cynically to the whole modernising, commercialising ethic of successive post-war governments. The exacerbated mood, however, spills over into a dismal and intolerant attitude to the crowd in the M1 café, whose 'kids are screaming for more'. Not surprisingly, perhaps, Larkin has often been portrayed as an arch conservative, and in an interview with the *Observer* in 1979 he was reported to have said 'I adore Mrs Thatcher' (Larkin, 1983, p.52). It would be extremely unwise, however, to read the poems in relation to that flippant remark. All of the poems in *High Windows* were completed long before Thatcherism was established as a political ideology. It is also worth noting R.L. Brett's revelation that Larkin's feelings of emptiness and depression 'grew as the Government's policy towards the universities threatened the future of the library he had built up and the university he had served for so long' (Brett, 1988, p.111).

While Larkin's later work is sometimes given to expressions of right-wing hostility, the abiding political tradition to which his poetry belongs is that of liberal humanism. The idea of the isolated individual surviving in an alien and fragmented society is a well-established liberal sentiment, and Larkin's characteristic response, like that of E.M. Forster, is to seek 'connection'. If the economic disarray of the late 1960s and early 1970s produces a poetry of profound disenchantment, it also leads to an increasing sense of communal obligation and commitment, and to a desire to rebuild and renew a sense of collective life. The opening poem in *High Windows*, 'To the Sea', establishes an emotional connection with the speaker's childhood outings. Stepping over the low wall above the shore 'Brings sharply back something known long before' (p.173). The family outings to the seaside represent for the speaker an image of unity and continuity in modern society: 'Still going on, all of it, still going on!' The disappearance of 'a white steamer stuck in the afternoon' signals the inevitable 'trek back', but the final stanza of the poem broadens into a moral commentary which recognises the annual seaside visit as both a pleasure and a sustaining ritual:

> The white steamer has gone. Like breathed-on glass
> The sunlight has turned milky. If the worst
> Of flawless weather is our falling short,
> It may be that through habit these do best,
> Coming to water clumsily undressed
> Yearly; teaching their children by a sort
> Of clowning; helping the old, too, as they ought.

In a similar way, 'Show Saturday' asserts the communal value of the annual agricultural show. The poem establishes its momentum by steadily gathering up the speaker's multiple impressions of an entire day's events. The sheer amount of detail contributes in a powerful way to the significance with which the show is invested in the final stanza. The example of Louis MacNeice continues to be a potent influence, and it is evident here in the alliterative, hyphenated assortment of people and things:

> The men with hunters, dog-breeding wool-defined women,
> Children all swaddle-swank, mugfaced middleaged wives
> Glaring at jellies, husbands on leave from the garden
> Watchful as weasels, car-tuning curt-haired sons –
> Back now, all of them, to their local lives . . .
>
> (p.200)

The degree of caricature in these lines makes the speaker's closing celebration of the show seem unexpected and all the more affirmative. The show provides a connection not just with an older England but with a primitive and organic force. This time it is earth, rather than water, that provides the elemental imagery: the show is like an annual plant that 'dies back into the area of work', and stays 'hidden there like strength'.

Significantly, the show has the power to counteract the 'Sale-bills and swindling' of the contemporary business ethic. The world of public finance is present in the juxtaposition of 'a Bank' with 'a beer-marquee', and in 'the quack of a man with pound notes round his hat', but 'Show Saturday' asserts a different kind of value: 'something they share / That breaks ancestrally each year into / Regenerate union'. Like 'To the Sea', the poem chooses an activity that exists at the margins of contemporary society, a 'miniature' way of life, as a means of recovering and restoring a lost sense of coherence and continuity. In that respect the poem does not have to contemplate the M1 cafés of 'Going, Going', though like the earlier poem it holds on to an England that is thought to be vanishing. The poem's vision of a shared and common culture is strongly willed but its scope is narrow and diminished. The closing statement, 'Let it always be there', is as much a plea as an assertion.

The need for integration and solidarity in *High Windows* is much more desperate and emphatic than in Larkin's earlier work. The same familiar technique of moving from spectatorial detachment to a shared predicament is at work in the poems, but the shifts in perspective are far more unsettling and intense. 'The Old Fools' opens with the brutal immediacy of Wilfred Owen's 'Mental Cases': 'What do they think has happened, the old fools, / To make them like this?' (p.196). Like Owen's poem, 'The Old Fools' proceeds to implicate its readers in a callous dismissal of impaired humanity, finally collapsing the distinction between 'them' and 'we'. The transition from repugnance to sympathetic identification occurs in stanza three, when the speaker tries to imagine the thoughts of old people. The poem's querulous rhetoric is stilled by a moment of heightened lyrical beauty:

> . . . sometimes only
> The rooms themselves, chairs and a fire burning,
> The blown bush at the window, or the sun's
> Faint friendliness on the wall some lonely
> Rain-ceased midsummer evening . . .

When the speaker returns to investigate the meaning of old age, it is with a terrified admission of fear and an alarming awareness of what remains unknown: 'Well, / We shall find out'.

'Vers de Société' challenges any easy distinction between creative solitude and social obligation, and like 'Old Fools' it succeeds in loosening and dispelling its own hardened attitudes. The poem opens with a crude dismissal of 'company': *My wife and I have asked a crowd of craps / To come and waste their time and ours: perhaps / You'd care to join us? In a pig's arse, friend.'* (p.181). The poem's change of heart is enabled by its slow modulation from the abrupt colloquial diction of stanza one into the more reflective, lyrical idiom of stanza three, with its more subdued recognition of solitude. Here we find the speaker sitting 'under a lamp' and 'looking out to see the moon thinned / To an air-sharpened blade'. The polite middle-class society of 'Warlock Williams' is made to appear as uninviting as possible, though finally it seems preferable to dwelling on 'failure and remorse'. Growing old makes companionship more urgent and desirable, but so too does the felt absence of God. It is Larkin's agnosticism that shapes the idea of sociability as a secular creed: 'the big wish / Is to have people nice to you'.

'Vers de Société' declares that 'Only the young can be alone freely', a sentiment that is echoed with generous compassion in 'Sad Steps'. Once again the speaker's reconciliation with 'others' is reinforced by the shift from a disgruntled colloquialism into a more serious and poignant lyricism. 'Groping back to bed after a piss', the speaker is startled by the appearance of the moon (p.169). The title, 'Sad Steps', is an allusion to sonnet XXXI of Sidney's *Astrophel and*

Stella: 'With how sad steps, O Moon, thou climbst the skies', though the poem also recalls Shelley's image of the moon 'Wandering companionless / Among the stars that have a different birth' ('To the Moon'). Larkin's poem, however, resists any tendency to exploit this literary currency or to romanticise the image of the moon. A symbolist idiom is invoked – 'Lozenge of love! Medallion of art!' – only to be firmly dismissed. The moral imperative, as so often in *High Windows*, outweighs the aesthetic:

> One shivers slightly, looking up there.
> The hardness and the brightness and the plain
> Far-reaching singleness of that wide stare
>
> Is a reminder of the strength and pain
> Of being young; that it can't come again,
> But is for others undiminished somewhere.

Larkin's characteristic technique of resting a positive assertion on a negative prefix is evident in the word 'undiminished', while 'somewhere' carries the same vague possibility that it does in the closing lines of 'The Whitsun Weddings'. Even so, the poem moves effectively from the isolated imagination to a sense of shared endeavour, refusing to accept literary stereotypes and intent on finding an appropriate contemporary language.

The unusual concentration on youth and age in *High Windows* is not just a consequence of 'the writer growing old'. As several poems make clear, the buoyant youthfulness of the 1960s highlights the disparities between one generation and the next. One of the most important factors in this respect was that new legislation on sexual issues led to attitudes that an older generation interpreted as 'permissiveness'. *High Windows* acknowledges a new and much freer discourse on sexual attitudes in its ironic tribute to the 1960s, 'Annus Mirabilis':

> Sexual intercourse began
> In nineteen sixty-three
> (Which was rather late for me) –
> Between the end of the *Chatterley* ban
> And the Beatles' first LP.
>
> (p.167)

The Latin title of the poem (mimicking John Dryden's poetic tribute to 1666) sets up expectations which are undercut by the burlesque opening stanza. Larkin's 'wonderful year' follows the famous 1960 trial for obscene publication (in which the jury decided D. H. Lawrence's *Lady Chatterley's Lover* could be published unexpurgated), and it anticipates the impact of pop culture with the release of *Please Please Me* by the Beatles in 1963. The poem's assertion that 'life was never better than / In nineteen sixty-three' is muted by the speaker's admission of having arrived 'too late', and also by the unconvincing rhetoric of the middle stanzas. The suggestion that 'life became / A brilliant breaking of the bank' is just one of a number of money metaphors in *High Windows* which offer a cynical response to the economic mismanagement of the decade.

'This Be The Verse' is an indication of how changing attitudes to sexuality permit a new form of colloquial address in Larkin's work. The poem is directed at the younger generation of the early 1970s and presents an uncompromising and unequivocal view of parenthood. The three rhyming quatrains offer a set of dismal and mordant reflections on sexuality, and yet the title is gleefully provocative. In a similar way, the sprightliness of the verse cuts against the severity of its sentiments, creating an unsettling, farcical mood. The closing stanza continues to denounce paternity but its attitude is more subdued and less risible than that of the preceding lines:

> Man hands on misery to man.
>   It deepens like a coastal shelf.
> Get out as early as you can
>   And don't have any kids yourself.

(p.180)

The image of misery deepening 'like a coastal shelf' is in keeping with the poem's flagrant renunciation of the biological process, but as the only simile in the poem it invites a more serious and sustained response. This slight rhetorical shift complicates interpretation and dissolves any easy distinction between ribald satire and underlying seriousness. 'It's perfectly serious' was Larkin's reply when told that the poem was 'funny' (Haffenden, 1981, p.128). 'This Be The Verse' is one of several poems in *High Windows* in which readers are confronted with severely partial viewpoints. In this respect the

poem might well be regarded as a critique of its own limited subjectivity, 'a splendid exposure of facile pessimism' (Lindop, 1980,
p.49).

'High Windows' is an ironic tribute to the sexual freedom of the
1960s, though its final lines lift it beyond irony into a more intense
and enigmatic idiom. The speaker's glib observation, 'I know this is
paradise', and his extravagant declaration of endless happiness
anticipate the poem's stylistic and rhetorical transition. Even so,
there are very few linguistic moments in Larkin's work so imposing
as that shift from the grim demotic of the opening lines, through the
jaundiced colloquialism of the penultimate stanza, to the poem's
final, luminous exaltation:

                              And immediately

Rather than words comes the thought of high windows:
The sun-comprehending glass,
And beyond it, the deep blue air, that shows
Nothing, and is nowhere, and is endless.

                                            (p.165)

The unusual modification of 'glass' as 'sun-comprehending' is an
oblique indication of what the speaker *cannot* know, in contrast to
the readily assumed 'I know this is paradise' in stanza one.
Similarly, the resounding endlessness of the final stanza contrasts
strongly with the clichéd remark about endless happiness in stanza
three. Like 'Here', 'High Windows' entertains the idea of a place
inaccessible to language, a place where ultimate meaning resides.
The remoteness of 'high windows' epitomises that distant imaginary
realm, but the intervening glass also marks the limits of vision. The
poem turns towards some bright element of existence but its final
lucent image is one of infinite yearning rather than transcendent
fulfilment.

What gives 'High Windows' its imposing modernity is not simply
its blunt colloquialism but its radical disjunction between word and
world. In that moment of transition between the final two stanzas,
the poem exposes its own vulnerability as a structure of language
and calls into question its own scope of reference. From a *poststructuralist* perspective, the writer's quest for transcendence or 'ultimate
meaning' is always impeded by the arbitrariness of language, by the

unstable relationship between *signifier* (the word) and what is *signified* (the meaning). One of the aims of *deconstruction* is to show how the written text strives to eradicate or conceal the gap between 'language' and the 'reality' it purports to embody. 'High Windows', however, openly declares the *absence* of any final referent or transcendental signification and confronts its readers with the concept of absolute zero. The explanation for this is to be found in Larkin's deep and abiding agnosticism. Poststructuralism recognises that the quest for 'full meaning' in language was originally postulated on a belief in the presence of God as the final guarantor of that meaning ('In the beginning was the Word'). In a strikingly modern fashion, Larkin's agnostic poetry reveals an explicit preoccupation with ideas of negation and emptiness.

Steve Clark makes the point that 'High Windows' 'starts out looking like a poem about sex, and becomes a poem about religion' (Clark, 1988, p.241), but the two are immediately implicated in the speaker's ironic invocation of 'paradise' in the opening stanza. There is a parallel throughout the poem between the sexual freedom of the new generation and the 'freethinking' agnosticism of the old: '*No God any more, or sweating in the dark / About hell and that ...*' In the event, both are revealed to be limited and illusory notions of freedom. Beyond the immediate concern with sex and religion, there is a political dimension to 'High Windows', about which Larkin himself is surprisingly frank: 'One longs for infinity and absence, the beauty of somewhere you're not. It shows humanity as a series of oppressions, and one wants to be somewhere where there's neither oppressed nor oppressor, just freedom' (Haffenden, 1981, p.127). It is in keeping with the liberal politics discussed in 'Fables of Freedom' (p.77) that Larkin should recognise 'oppression' and yet conceive of freedom in individual, imaginative terms. At the same time, however, Larkin's admission that 'one longs for infinity and absence' sits oddly alongside an earlier remark in the same interview: 'I don't want to transcend the commonplace, I love the commonplace' (Haffenden, 1981, p.124). This tension between commitment and disengagement is at its most acute in *High Windows*. As the fragile post-war consensus begins to break down, Larkin's poetry is increasingly caught between a liberal perception of oppressed humanity and an agnostic apprehension of infinite nothingness.

It is an alliance of liberal humanism and agnostic sentiment that

gives 'The Building' such a commanding presence in *High Windows*.
Here the oppression and the nothingness appear to be reconciled in
the sure assertion that 'All know they are going to die' (p.192). This
is the final consensus, in a place where humans are 'caught / On
ground curiously neutral, homes and names / Suddenly in abeyance
...'. The hospital in Larkin's poem has appropriated much of the
historical and social significance of the church in contending with
ceaseless death: 'All round it close-ribbed streets rise and fall / Like
a great sigh out of the last century'. At the same time, one of the
most striking aspects of the poem is its stylistic shift between the
quotidian surfaces of contemporary society and existential despair.
The speaker looks down from the hospital to the 'outside' world
where someone walks 'free':

> Then, past the gate,
> Traffic; a locked church; short terraced streets
> Where kids chalk games, and girls with hair-dos fetch
>
> Their separates from the cleaners – O world,
> Your loves, your chances, are beyond the stretch
> Of any hand from here!

The reference to a locked church suggests the extent to which the
secular administering of the hospital has superseded the spiritual
rites of the church. At the same time, whatever significance the
hospital might acquire in the late twentieth century, 'unless its
powers / Outbuild cathedrals nothing contravenes / The coming
dark'. Similarly, we are reminded in 'Aubade' of 'The anaesthetic
from which none come round' (p.208). Like Louis MacNeice's
'Aubade for Infants', Larkin's dawn-song subverts the usual joyful
associations of the genre by asking 'what things befall?' Once again,
the radical agnosticism in Larkin's work manifests itself in a poetics
of absence, in a startling realisation of total emptiness: 'The sure
extinction that we travel to / And shall be lost in always'. But as
with 'The Building', it is not just the way in which the language of
the poem articulates emptiness that characterises these late poems;
it is also their recognition and understanding of such fear in terms of
a contemporary social context, where 'telephones crouch, getting
ready to ring / In locked-up offices', and where 'Postmen like
doctors go from house to house'.

The end of consensus and the increasingly divisive social and
political views that ensued had a significant shaping effect on
Larkin's later poems, not least in the degree of ethical relativism
which they display. *High Windows* shows an unusual interest in
moments of historical change or imagined scenes from the past.
Such poems as 'The Card-Players', 'How Distant' and, most
importantly, 'Livings', explore the values and belief systems of
contrasting social groups, but also reach back in the search for
something elemental and enduring in human existence. As Roger
Day has argued, 'The Card-Players' is 'a verbal *tableau vivant* from
a former century, an enactment of an interior scene painted by a
Dutch Old Master' (Day, 1987, p.66). The names and actions of its
card-players parody this kind of painting, but also establish a
correspondence between human and natural elements: Jan van
Hogspeuw 'pisses at the dark', Dirk Dogstoerd 'holds a cinder to his
clay with tongs', and Old Prijck 'snores with the gale' (p.177). The
final line recognises this existence as grotesque and elemental and
yet celebrates its sublime power: 'Rain, wind and fire! The secret,
bestial peace!'. 'The Card-Players' is an imaginative realisation of a
seemingly untroubled world view and way of life, now lost beneath
'Wet century-wide trees'. The poem's overtly parodic technique,
however, ensures that this contented 'bestial peace' is regarded as
no more than a fictional perspective, already mediated through art.
As Guido Latré suggests, 'the speaker has formulated the raw
experiences of the card-players themselves in the sophisticated
poetic form of a sonnet, thus emphasizing the enormous gap
between the situation of his own discourse and that of the Dutch-
men'. Accordingly, the poem acknowledges 'an experience from
which the whole civilized world of the twentieth century is alienated'
(Latré, 1985, pp.281–2). In a similar way, 'How Distant' recalls
the emigration of young labourers at the turn of the century in vivid,
imaginative detail, only to recognise what is past and gone:

> This is being young,
> Assumption of the startled century
>
> Like new store clothes,
> The huge decisions printed out by feet
> Inventing where they tread,
> The random windows conjuring a street.

(p.162)

The title is an emphatic insistence upon what is now irrecoverable and yet that qualifying 'How' also induces a powerful sense of loss and melancholy. As with 'The Card-Players', the poem's continuous present tense holds out the alluring possibility of 'starting over again'.

'Livings' juxtaposes two world views that are about to be shattered – that of an agricultural salesman in the late 1920s and that of a Cambridge don in the late seventeenth century – and between them it places the turbulent, elemental existence of a lighthouse keeper. The resulting triptych presents a series of contrasting perspectives and lifestyles. The word 'Livings' catches both the plurality of these lifestyles and their present-tense perspective: each voice takes on the dramatic and conversational effects of a soliloquy. The salesman in 'Livings' I talks of 'Government tariffs, wages, price of stock' (p.186). Business goes on, but there is an undercurrent of unease in the image of a splendid sunset over the river and the Customs House working late into the evening. Drowsing between his 'ex-Army sheets' and regarding the pictures of the trenches as 'stuff / Nobody minds or notices', the speaker cannot predict the tumultuous events of the 1930s. His closing line is tragically understated: 'It's time for change, in nineteen twenty-nine'. Just as the salesman's language evokes a lost decade – 'The boots carries my lean old leather case' – so 'Livings' III employs such words as 'advowson' (an application for a Church 'living' or property), 'jordan' (a chamber-pot) and 'sizar' (a Cambridge University student paying reduced fees and originally having menial duties to perform). Once again, life goes on amid the topics of the day: 'Dusty shelves hold prayers and proofs' (of God's existence) and 'Chaldean constellations' (as determined by ancient astrology) 'Sparkle over crowded roofs'. The insistent present-tense evocation of a secure world view and a social order renewed after 'regicide' is heightened by a twentieth-century reader's retrospective knowledge of change and loss. Contrasting with the extensive social dealings of 'Livings' I and III is the solitary figure of the lighthouse keeper, buffeted by the elements and yet 'Guarded by brilliance', forecasting events with divining-cards. Alan Brownjohn points out that the lighthouse keeper's 'living' can be likened to 'the poet's precarious vantage point', with 'the lighthouse symbolizing both creativity and intense loneliness' (Brownjohn, 1975, p.19).

Larkin's evident fascination with the poignant details of outmoded lifestyles and his corresponding search for something 'elemental' is perhaps best understood in terms of an increasing sense of alienation amidst the economic and political disarray of the late 1960s and early 1970s. One of the most obvious forms that this alienation takes is a deep repugnance for the crudely exploitative modern economy and a seeming reverence for the older mercantile civilisation typified in 'Livings' I. Anxieties about a culture seemingly dominated by 'money' pervade the later poems, as we have already seen in the discussion of 'Homage to a Government' and 'Going, Going'. Jake Balokowsky, the disreputable researcher in 'Posterity', 'makes the money sign' (p.170), and the speaker in 'The Building' reflects on human illness and 'how much money goes / In trying to correct it' (p.191). In brilliant contrast, however, is the elemental exchange and pure gold of the sun in 'Solar':

> Coined there among
> Lonely horizontals
> You exist openly.
> Our needs hourly
> Climb and return like angels.
> Unclosing like a hand,
> You give for ever.
>
> (p.159)

In 'Friday Night in the Royal Station Hotel' the radiance of 'Solar' has vanished and 'Light spreads darkly downwards from the high / Clusters of lights over empty chairs' (p.163). The poem conveys its profound sense of 'exile' in terms of the absence and emptiness that seem to linger in a large hotel after 'all the salesmen have gone back to Leeds'. Again, the impulse is to let the imagination dwell on something elemental, but the mood of exile cannot be dispelled: *'Night comes on. Waves fold behind villages'*. It is a sign of the enduring legacy of 1930s poetry that, in registering its feelings of social dislocation, 'Friday Night in the Royal Station Hotel' should return so intently and alertly to the example of W.H. Auden.

If 'Solar' represents Larkin's purest ideal of giving and receiving, the poem simply titled 'Money' is the quintessential statement of alienation:

> Quarterly, is it, money reproaches me:
>   'Why do you let me lie here wastefully?
> I am all you never had of goods and sex.
>   You could get them still by writing a few cheques.'

The rhythmic banality of 'sex' and 'cheques' and the verbal flatness of 'had' and 'get' convey a liberal distaste for the crude exchange mechanism of the modern economy. The speaker's sarcastic under-statement quietly demystifies the power of money as he turns to enquire what other people 'do with theirs': 'By now they've a second house and car and wife: / Clearly money has something to do with life' (p.198). As with 'High Windows', the poem moves from the drollery of its middle stanzas into a sublimation of its own worldly anxieties:

> I listen to money singing. It's like looking down
>   From long french windows at a provincial town,
> The slums, the canal, the churches ornate and mad
>   In the evening sun. It is intensely sad.

The siren temptations of money evoke in the speaker a chronic sense of cultural melancholy. The light of the evening sun, as in 'Livings' I, transmits an aura of social decline, a shadowing of civilisation. The speaker looks *down* from an imaginative, artistic perspective at the provincial town with its slums and canal. The context is one in which material and spiritual aspirations are grossly confused. The churches appear defunct and unreal, having a merely decorative appeal. There are very few twentieth-century poems that catch so well the dissenting spirit of the young Karl Marx, writing in 1843:

> Money is the universal, self-constituted value of all things. It has therefore robbed the whole world, human as well as natural, of its own values. Money is the alienated essence of man's work and being, this alien essence dominates him and he adores it. (McLellan, 1988, p.60)

The closing stanza of 'Money' employs a self-conscious and seem-ingly incongruous poetic simile – 'It's like looking down . . .' – as a way of reasserting the role of the imagination in a modern civilisation that appears increasingly hollow and deprived of value. The poem's intensity of feeling is a measure of that absence and emptiness.

High Windows is a work of political liberalism, not Marxism, and yet its mood of dissent is so powerful and sustained that it cannot help but reveal the essential contradiction in a society that asserts the need for human community at one level and stresses the need for competition at another. Such poems as 'Money' and 'Friday Night in the Royal Station Hotel' acknowledge those pressures which give rise to isolation and alienation, to the desire for solitariness and transcendence. In other poems such as 'To the Sea' and 'Show Saturday', however, there is a strong commitment to the ideal of a common culture, and a desire for integration within communal life. Raymond Williams has pointed to the tragic dimensions of this division of experience into personal and social categories (the individual *against* society rather than the individual *within* society) and has referred to it as 'the deepest crisis in modern literature':

> From this recognition, there is no way out, within the liberal consciousness. There is either the movement to common desire, common aspiration, which politically is socialism, or there is acceptance, reluctant at first but strengthening and darkening, of failure and breakdown as common and inevitable. (Williams, 1966, pp.101–2)

Larkin's 'Vers de Société' recognises the terms of this crisis and shows a defensive sarcasm collapsing in its midst: 'Beyond the light stand failure and remorse' (p.182). Many of the poems in *High Windows* are rhetorically offensive and overtly didactic, such is their need for human contact and sustaining relationships, while others bleakly contemplate extinction. Two of Larkin's later poems, however, are characterised by an intense elegiac lyricism. 'Dublinesque' and 'The Explosion' were written within six months of each other in the early part of 1970, and both are concerned with moments of grief and loss within working-class communities. The imaginative release in these poems is not into some lucent, nihilistic element, but into a vision of communal solidarity, into a generous awareness of human resilience and shared endeavour. There is no conflict in these poems between 'the individual' and 'society' or between the disillusioned intelligence of the poet and the imposing demands of other people.

These are poems which are profoundly imaginative but also profoundly engaged with social ideals and beliefs. In the end, the values of Larkin's poetry are deeply in opposition to the relentless monetarism and economic individualism that came to dominate the late 1970s and 1980s.

'Dublinesque' and 'The Explosion' are vivid renderings of late nineteenth- or early twentieth-century life and are reminiscent of prose works by Joyce and Lawrence respectively. 'Dublinesque', as its title suggests, is a distillation or evocation of the spirit of Dublin, and a sense of distance and antiquity is conveyed through the atmospheric details of 'pewter' light and 'afternoon mist' (p.178). The poem's preoccupation with Irish cultural identity is evident in the alliterative alignment of 'race-guides and rosaries'. The opening stanza recedes 'Down stucco sidestreets', as if slipping back in history, but emerges in the immediate present tense: 'A funeral passes'. The occasion is one of tremendous communal endeavour and the poem emphasises the resourcefulness and vitality of the people, both in what their clothing suggests – mournful respect but continuing cheerfulness – and in the unifying image of the dance: skirts are held 'skilfully' and 'Someone claps time'. The essential mood of the occasion is caught by the enlarging, ennobling effect of the repetition in 'great friendliness . . . great sadness'. The emotional impact of the event is felt most acutely, however, in the slowly diminishing perspective of the closing lines:

> As they wend away
> A voice is heard singing
> Of Kitty, or Katy,
> As if the name meant once
> All love, all beauty.

That final, poignant detail of the name – was it Kitty or Katy? – recalls an earlier preoccupation with the naming powers of language (in such poems as 'At Grass' and 'Maiden Name') and with the mysterious way in which names come to embody a lost plenitude of meaning ('*All* love, *all* beauty'). 'Dublinesque', however, exerts a much more radical poetics of absence. The splitting signifiers of 'the name', the conditional verbal tense and the irrevocable 'once' all point to the deep divide between word and world, and show language at the extreme edge of meaning. The persistence of that singing 'voice' is a reassertion of imaginative vitality in the face of negation, a reminder of the abundance of life amidst the presence of death.

It might seem surprising in view of the right-wing hostility that invades such poems as 'Going, Going' and 'Homage to a Government' that *High Windows* should locate its lost sense of value in images of working-class solidarity. In the end, however, there is nowhere else for the beleaguered liberal consciousness to turn, and it seems highly appropriate that Larkin should have chosen for the final page of *High Windows* an elegiac tribute to the victims of a mining disaster. R.P. Draper has tried to incorporate 'The Explosion' within a tradition of 'lyric tragedy' characterised by Milton's 'Lycidas': 'The Christianised pastoral elegy, which looks beyond suffering to the resurrection and exaltation of the dead, is given a new and strangely beautiful variation' (Draper, 1985, p.214). But as Peter Hollindale has argued in his excellent analysis of the poem, there are two other prominent literary sources in 'The Explosion': *The Song of Hiawatha* by Henry Wadsworth Longfellow and the English ballad or folk song tradition. The significance of the *Hiawatha* metre is that it allows momentous events to be absorbed within 'a verbal and experiential rhythm of continuity which makes them bearable' (Hollindale, 1989, p.141). Along with this buoyant, sustaining rhythm there is a profusion and accumulation of random detail: 'Fathers, brothers, nicknames, laughter'. There is also the unusual syntactic device of *The Song of Hiawatha*, by which verbal gestures in the past are complemented by present tense participles to create an effect of continuing action. The most important relationship here is between the two verbs linking the image of the lark's eggs – 'showed' and 'showing' – since it signifies the transition not only from life to death but from 'commonplace to supernatural marvel' (Hollindale, 1989, p.145).

The local details, such as 'beards and moleskins', link the poem to the nineteenth-century industrial ballad, while the plain lettering in the chapels suggests that the context is one of nonconformist working-class religion. It is the interplay of the song-like rhythm and the narrative element of the disaster ballad that makes the poem's presentation of events seem so sublime and strangely disconcerting. Eight triplets are followed by the single revelatory closing line. The italicised sixth stanza catches the drift of the 'plain' sermon, but it is an unshakeable belief in these words that enables the vision of resurrection that follows:

> Plain as lettering in the chapels
> It was said, and for a second
> Wives saw men of the explosion
>
> Larger than in life they managed –
> Gold as on a coin, or walking
> Somehow from the sun towards them,
>
> One showing the eggs unbroken.

From the opening stanza onwards, the sun is a controlling image in the poem and, as in 'Solar', it exists as a pure, life-giving force. The phrase 'Gold as on a coin' is a reminder of how insistently the poems in *High Windows* seeks an enduring value beyond the crude exchange of money. The amazement of 'walking / Somehow from the sun' is another instance of that cautiously indefinite vocabulary that characterises Larkin's agnostic poetry, but the final line with its fragile, touching detail of the lark's eggs is an unqualified affirmation of the instinct for shared protection and mutual survival in working-class communities.

To read Philip Larkin's poetry historically, then, is not to read it in terms of the accuracy or verisimilitude with which it embodies a particular historical moment. As we have seen, many of the poems are imagined re-creations of distant ways of life which often expose and undermine their own claims to 'realism'. Nor is it a matter of reading the poems in terms of the writer's personal history. For all the declared conservatism of the man himself, the political nature of the poetry is often complex and contradictory. To read a work historically is not to consign it to the past but to realise its potential in the present; to read it, that is, in terms of how it might transform our knowledge of the past and therefore our understanding of the present. In this respect, the abiding concern of historicist criticism is not with a history that is past and gone but with a history that is still being lived. As new horizons of reading and new critical perspectives continue to unfold, it seems likely that many readers will come to regard the poetry of Philip Larkin as an imaginative declaration of resistance and solidarity against the aggressive and demeaning self-interest that has characterised the final decades of the twentieth century.

References

Alvarez, A. (ed.), *The New Poetry* (Harmondsworth, 1962; 1966).

Ayer, Alfred Jules, *Language, Truth and Logic* (London, 1946; 1960).

Barnett, Correlli, *The Collapse of British Power* (London, 1972).

Barthes, Roland, *Writing Degree Zero* (London, 1967).

Bedient, Calvin, *Eight Contemporary Poets* (London, 1974).

Brett, R.L., 'Philip Larkin in Hull', in Hartley (1988), p.111.

Brown, Merle, *Double Lyric: Divisiveness and Communal Creativity in Recent English Poetry* (London, 1980).

Brownjohn, Alan, *Philip Larkin* (London, 1975).

Carter, Ronald (ed.), *Language and Literature: An Introductory Reader in Stylistics* (London, 1982).

Clark, Steve, 'Get Out As Early As You Can: Larkin's Sexual Politics', in Hartley (1988), pp.237–71.

Conquest, Robert (ed.), *New Lines: An Anthology* (London, 1956).

Conquest, Robert (ed.), *New Lines – II: An Anthology* (London, 1963).

Cookson, Linda and Brian Loughrey, *Critical Essays on Philip Larkin: The Poems* (Harlow, 1989).

Cox, C.B., 'Philip Larkin', *Critical Quarterly*, 1 (1959), 14–17.

Cox, C.B. and A.E. Dyson, *Modern Poetry: Studies in Practical Criticism* (London, 1963).

Crozier, Andrew, 'Thrills and frills: poetry as figures of empirical lyricism', in Sinfield (1983), pp.199–233.

Day, Roger, *Larkin* (Milton Keynes, 1987).

Day, Roger, '"That vast moth-eaten musical brocade": Larkin and religion', in Cookson and Loughrey (1989), pp.81–92.

Davie, Donald, 'Landscapes of Larkin', in *Thomas Hardy and British Poetry* (London, 1973), pp.63–82.

Delaney, Shelagh, *A Taste of Honey* (London, 1956; 1987).

Dodsworth, Martin (ed.), *The Survival of Poetry* (London, 1970).

Dollimore, Jonathan, *Radical Tragedy* (Brighton, 1984).

Draper, R.P., 'Philip Larkin: "the bone's truth"', in *Lyric Tragedy* (London, 1985).

Dunn, Douglas, *Under the Influence: Douglas Dunn on Philip Larkin* (Edinburgh, 1987).

Enright, D.J. (ed.), *Poets of the 1950s: An Anthology of New English Verse* (Tokyo, 1955).

Everett, Barbara, 'Philip Larkin: After Symbolism', *Essays in Criticism*, XXX (1980), 227–42. Reprinted in *Poets in their Time* (London, 1986), pp.230–44.

Everett, Barbara, 'Larkin's Edens', in *Poets in their Time* (London, 1986), pp.245–57.

Falck, Colin, 'Philip Larkin', in Hamilton (1968), pp.101–10.

Ford, Boris (ed.), *The Pelican Guide to English Literature, Vol. 7: The Modern Age* (Harmondsworth, 1973).

Fowler, Roger, *Literature as Social Discourse: The Practice of Linguistic Criticism* (Bloomington, Indiana, 1981).

Fraser, G.S. and Ian Fletcher (eds), *Springtime: An Anthology of Young Poets and Writers* (London, 1953).

Gibson, James (ed.), *Let the Poet Choose* (London, 1973).

Goodby, John, '"The importance of elsewhere", or "No man is an Ireland": self, selves and social consensus in the poetry of Philip Larkin', *Critical Survey*, 1 (1989), 131–8.

Goode, John, 'A Reading of Deceptions', in Hartley (1988), pp.126–34.

Grubb, Frederick, *A Vision of Reality: A Study of Liberalism in Twentieth-Century Verse* (London, 1965).

Haffenden, John (ed.), *Viewpoints: Poets in Conversation* (London, 1981).

Hamilton, Ian (ed.), *The Modern Poet: Essays from the Review* (London, 1968).

Hamilton, Ian, 'The Making of the Movement', in Schmidt and Lindop (1972), pp.70–3.

Hartley, Anthony, 'Poets of the Fifties', *Spectator*, 27 August 1954, pp.260–1.

Hartley, Anthony, *A State of England* (London, 1963).

Hartley, George (ed.), *Philip Larkin 1922–1985: A Tribute* (London, 1988).

Hartley, Jean, *Philip Larkin, The Marvell Press and Me* (Manchester, 1989).

Heaney, Seamus, 'Englands of the Mind', in *Preoccupations: Selected Prose 1968–78* (London, 1980), pp.150–69.

Heaney, Seamus, 'The Main of Light', in Thwaite (1982), pp.131–8. Reprinted in *The Government of the Tongue* (London, 1988), pp.15–22.

Hewison, Robert, *In Anger: Culture in the Cold War 1945–60* (London, 1981).

Hobsbaum, Philip, 'Larkin's Singing Line', in Hartley (1988), pp.284–92.

Holbrook, David, *Lost Bearings in English Poetry* (London, 1977).

Holderness, Graham, 'Reading "Deceptions" – a dramatic conversation', *Critical Survey*, 1 (1989), 122–9.

Holderness, Graham, 'Philip Larkin: the limits of experience', in Cookson and Loughrey (1989), pp.106–14.

Hollindale, Peter, 'Philip Larkin's "The Explosion"', *Critical Survey*, 1 (1989), 139–48.

Hynes, Samuel, 'Sweeping the Empty Stage' (Review of Morrison, 1980), *Times Literary Supplement*, 20 June 1980, p.699.

James, Clive, 'Don Juan in Hull: Philip Larkin', in *At the Pillars of Hercules* (London, 1979), pp.51–72.

Jameson, Fredric, *Modernism and Imperialism* (Derry, 1988).

Jauss, Hans Robert, *Toward an Aesthetic of Reception* (Brighton, 1982).

Jones, Alun R., 'The Poetry of Philip Larkin', *Western Humanities Review*, XVI (1962), 143–52.

Jones, Peter and Michael Schmidt (eds), *British Poetry Since 1970: A Critical Survey* (Manchester, 1980).

Kuby, Lolette, *An Uncommon Poet for the Common Man: A Study of Philip Larkin's Poetry* (The Hague, 1974).

Larkin, Philip, *Required Writing: Miscellaneous Pieces 1955–1982* (London, 1983).

Latré, Guido, *Locking Earth to the Sky: A Structuralist Approach to Philip Larkin's Poetry* (Frankfurt am Main, 1985).

Lindop, Grevel, 'Being different from yourself: Philip Larkin in the 1970s', in Jones and Schmidt (1980), pp.46–54.

Lodge, David, 'Philip Larkin: The Metonymic Muse', in *The Modes of Modern Writing: Metaphor, Metonymy, and the Typology of Modern Literature* (London, 1977), pp.118–28.

Longley, Edna, 'Larkin, Edward Thomas and the Tradition',

Phoenix, 11–12 (1973/4), pp.63–89. Reprinted as '"Any-angled light": Philip Larkin and Edward Thomas', in *Poetry in the Wars* (Newcastle, 1986), pp.113–39.

Longley, Edna, 'Poète Maudit Manqué', in Hartley (1988), pp.220–31.

Lucas, John, *Modern English Poetry From Hardy to Hughes* (London, 1986).

Martin, Bruce K., *Philip Larkin* (Boston, 1978).

Marwick, Arthur, *British Society Since 1945* (Harmondsworth, 1986).

McLellan, David, *Karl Marx: Selected Writings* (Oxford, 1988).

Morgan, Edwin, *Sovpoems* (Worcester, 1961).

Morgan, Kenneth, *The People's Peace: British History 1945–1989* (Oxford, 1990).

Morrison, Blake, *The Movement: English Poetry and Fiction of the 1950s* (Oxford, 1980).

Morrison, Blake, 'In the Grip of Darkness', *Times Literary Supplement*, 14–20 October 1988, pp.1151–2.

Motion, Andrew, and Blake Morrison, *The Penguin Book of Contemporary British Poetry* (Harmondsworth, 1982).

Motion, Andrew, *Philip Larkin* (London, 1982).

O'Neill, Michael, 'The Importance of Difference: Larkin's *The Whitsun Weddings*', in Hartley (1988), pp.184–97.

Osborne, John, 'The Hull Poets', *Bête Noire*, 2/3 (1987), 180–204.

Paulin, Tom, *Thomas Hardy: The Poetry of Perception* (London, 1975; 1986).

Paulin, Tom, 'Into the Heart of Englishness', *Times Literary Supplement*, 20–26 July 1990, pp.779–80.

Petch, Simon, *The Art of Philip Larkin* (Sydney, 1981).

Pinkney, Tony, 'Old Toads Down Cemetery Road', *News From Nowhere*, 1 (1986), 37–47.

Porter, Peter, 'Philip Larkin: the Making of a Master', *The Independent*, 8 October 1988.

Press, John, *Rule and Energy: Trends in British Poetry Since the Second World War* (London, 1963).

Press, John, *A Map of Modern English Verse* (London, 1969).

Raban, Jonathan, *The Society of the Poem* (London, 1971).

Ricks, Christopher, 'The Whitsun Weddings', *Phoenix*, 11–12 (1973/4), pp.6–10.

Rorty, Richard, *Contingency, irony, and solidarity* (Cambridge, 1989).

Rosenthal, M.L., *The Modern Poets: A Critical Introduction* (New York, 1965).

Rosenthal, M.L., *The New Poets: American and British Poetry Since World War II* (New York, 1967).

Samuel, Raphael (ed.), *Patriotism: The Making and Unmaking of British National Identity, Volume I: History and Politics* (London, 1989).

Scott, J.D., 'In the Movement', *Spectator*, 1 October 1954, pp.399–400.

Schmidt, Michael and Grevel Lindop (eds), *British Poetry Since 1960: A Critical Survey* (Oxford, 1972).

Sergeant, Howard and Dannie Abse (eds), *Mavericks: An Anthology* (London, 1957).

Sinfield, Alan (ed.), *Society and Literature 1945–1970* (London, 1983).

Sinfield, Alan, *Literature, Politics and Culture in Postwar Britain* (Oxford, 1989).

Smith, Stan, *Inviolable Voice: History and Twentieth-Century Poetry* (Dublin, 1982).

Stannard, Martin, 'The Men Running up to Bowl: Aspects of Stasis in the Work of Larkin and Amis', *Ideas and Production*, IX–X (1989), pp.45–56.

Thwaite, Anthony, 'The Poetry of Philip Larkin', in Dodsworth (1970), pp.37–55.

Thwaite, Anthony (ed.), *Larkin at Sixty* (London, 1982).

Timms, David, *Philip Larkin* (Edinburgh, 1973).

Tomlinson, Charles, 'The Middlebrow Muse' (Review of Conquest, 1956), *Essays in Criticism*, VII (1957), 208–17.

Tomlinson, Charles, 'Poetry Today', in Ford (1973), pp.471–89.

Trotter, David, *The Making of the Reader: Language and Subjectivity in Modern American, English and Irish Poetry* (London, 1984).

Underhill, Hugh, 'Poetry of departures: Larkin and the power of choosing', *Critical Survey*, 1 (1989), 183–93.

Wain, John, 'The Poetry of Philip Larkin', *Malahat Review*, 39 (1976), 95–112.

Walcott, Derek, 'The Master of the Ordinary', *New York Review of Books*, 1 June 1989, pp.37–40.

Walsh, Martin J., *A History of Philosophy* (London, 1985).

Watson, J.R., 'The Other Larkin', *Critical Quarterly*, 17 (1975), 347–60.

Watson, J.R., 'Clichés and common speech in Philip Larkin's poetry', *Critical Survey*, 1 (1989), 149–63.

Whalen, Terry, *Philip Larkin and English Poetry* (London, 1986).

Widdowson, H.G., 'The Conditional Presence of Mr Bleaney', in Carter (1982), pp.19–26.

Williams, Raymond, *Modern Tragedy* (London, 1966).

Index